THE INFLUENCE OF HUDSON TAYLOR ON THE
FAITH MISSIONS MOVEMENT

by

Daniel W. Bacon

B.A., Whitworth College, 1962
Th.M., Dallas Theological Seminary, 1966

A MAJOR PROJECT

Submitted to the Faculty
in partial fulfillment of the requirements
for the degree
DOCTOR OF MISSIOLOGY
at Trinity Evangelical Divinity School

Deerfield, Illinois
June 1983

First published 1984

ISBN 9971-972-03-4

OMF BOOKS are distributed by
OMF, 404 South Church Street,
Robesonia, Pa. 19551, USA, and
OMF, Belmont, The Vine,
Sevenoaks, Kent, TN13 3TZ, UK
and other OMF offices.

Published by Overseas Missionary Fellowship (IHQ) Ltd,
2 Cluny Road, Singapore 1025, Republic of Singapore,
and printed by Hiap Seng Press Pte. Ltd, Singapore.

PREFACE TO SERIES

How often have you longed to dig into those
stacks of research papers and theses written by students
of missions? Hard earned lessons of experience and even
masses of research data are often repeated again and
again because few people knew of their experience.

The Overseas Missionary Fellowship has decided
to tackle this problem by publishing the OMF BOOKS STUDY
SERIES. These books will be the result of important
study projects related to OMF and its ministry that are
considered relevant to others.

Cost is often as big as problem as accessibility.
We are therefore publishing this series in an attractive
yet inexpensive format.

Our prayer is that you will profit from these
studies and that together we will see our Lord's commission
fulfilled.

Stuart R Imbach

OMF Communications Department

ABOUT THE AUTHOR

Daniel W. Bacon is a graduate of Whitworth
College and Dallas Theological Seminary. He joined the
Overseas Missionary Fellowship in 1967 and has served in
Japan where he was involved in a church-planting ministry,
and in Singapore at the Mission's International
Headquarters. Since 1978 he has been Home Director for
OMF in the USA.

TABLE OF CONTENTS

PART I. THE MISSIOLOGICAL DISTINCTIVES
OF HUDSON TAYLOR AND THE
CHINA INLAND MISSION

Chapter

PART I

THE MISSIOLOGICAL DISTINCTIVES

OF HUDSON TAYLOR AND THE

CHINA INLAND MISSION

CHAPTER I

HISTORICAL BACKGROUND

J. Hudson Taylor has become a household word in missions. Down
through the years thousands of Christians have been touched by Taylor's
life, work and spiritual legacy. Many of these have been caught up in
the worldwide missionary task to which Taylor gave such inspired leadership during his generation. Not only individuals, but many Christian
missions and institutions incorporated principles and patterns which
grew out of Hudson Taylor's founding of the China Inland Mission and
his missionary statesmanship for nearly half a century.

Hudson Taylor has been variously portrayed as a model worthy of
imitation by Christians and would-be missionaries. For many, Taylor's
character and spiritual life have become challenges and incentives to
deeper faith and commitment. Interestingly, J. Hudson Taylor, although
a radical strategist, is remembered more as a man of God and a source of
spiritual inspiration than as a missiologist.[1]

And yet from a missiological viewpoint, Taylor has been and
still is impacting the world of missions. The church historian,
Professor K. S. Latourette, has described Taylor as "one of the greatest

_____

[1]Dr. and Mrs. Howard Taylor, J. Hudson Taylor: God's Man in
China (Chicago: Moody Press, 1965), Foreword.

1

missionaries of all time."[2] Latourette went on to state of Hudson

Taylor that "the repercussions of his daring faith were to be felt,

not only in the vast country to which he gave himself, but also in

many lands."[3] Indeed, the impact of Taylor and the China Inland Mission

which he founded has been far wider than this nineteenth

century pioneer could have dreamed. Through Hudson Taylor's

inspiration numbers of other faith missions were spawned, and in the

words of Dr. Ralph Winter, "Taylor became the founder of a new era in

missions."[4] Thus, in an act of faith and obedience to the call of

God for the evangelization of inland China's unreached millions,

Taylor unwittingly became ". . . the father of the faith mission

movement. . . ."[5]

China and Nineteenth Century Missions

No life is lived in a vacuum. This was certainly true of

Hudson Taylor and the work which he accomplished. Although Taylor is

often described as a radical thinker, innovator and pacesetter in

missions, yet a multitude of forces were at work molding and guiding

the direction of his life and shaping his missionary vision and

---

[2]K. S. Latourette, A History of Christian Missions in China
(New York: Macmillan Co., 1929), p. 328.

[3]A. J. Broomhall, Hudson Taylor and China's Open Century:
If I Had a Thousand Lives, Book III (London: Hodder and Stoughton
and the Overseas Missionary Fellowship, 1982), p. 441.

[4]Ralph D. Winter and Steven C. Hawthorne, eds., Perspectives On
The World Christian Movement: A Reader (Pasadena: William Carey
Library, 1981), p. 172.

[5]J. Herbert Kane, A Concise History of the Christian World
Mission: A Panoramic View of Missions from Pentecost to the Present
(Grand Rapids: Baker Book House, 1978), p. 96.

subsequent policies for his mission. As Taylor came to influence many in new directions, so was he also the product of many influences.

China in the mid-nineteenth century was seen as a land of opportunity and perplexity to most Westerners. Attempts to establish free trade with China had been steadily resisted, and only through gunboat diplomacy had the nation reluctantly opened its doors for interchange with foreign agencies. With the signing of the treaties of 1842-44, Catholic and Protestant missionaries sought to take advantage of the new diplomatic climate and the opening of the five ports of Canton, Amoy, Fuchow, Ningpo, and Shanghai to foreign trade.[6] While the Catholic church was reacting quickly to the new opportunities, Protestant churches lagged far behind in interest or awareness of the situation.

A. J. Broomhall characterizes this period when he says:

> The total number of Protestant missionaries to the Chinese in East Asia was fifty, not including wives. In India there were in 1851 some ninety-one thousand Protestant Christian adherents, of whom fewer than fifteen thousand were communicant members of the church. . . . But the grand total of Chinese Protestant Christians was only about two hundred, and most of them were in Malaysia. Forty-five years after Morrison began at Canton success seemed as remote as ever.[7]

Thus China's vast population of almost 400 million was still untouched, unevangelized, and worse still, unnoticed by churches in the West.

The very size of China--both in geographical vastness and in the complexity of the political, cultural and social situation--made the task of evangelization more than formidable. Prior to Taylor's

---

[6]A. J. Broomhall, Hudson Taylor and China's Open Century: Over The Treaty Wall, Book II (London: Hodder and Stoughton and the Overseas Missionary Fellowship, 1982), p. 21.

[7]Ibid., p. 22.

arrival in China, other Protestant missionaries had been valiantly
seeking ways of introducing the gospel, and Hudson Taylor learned
from them and built upon their efforts and insights. Much credit must
be given to Robert Morrison, who translated the Scriptures in Chinese.
Others like Walter Medhurst also helped prepare the way through the
production of large amounts of Christian literature in Chinese.
Dr. Peter Parker through missionary medicine opened many hearts in the
Canton area. Some like Elijah Bridgman and Samuel Wells Williams
through their Chinese Repository and other publications helped to create
a greater climate of mutual understanding between Westerners
and Chinese.[8]

One of the most significant pioneers to China and of special
influence on Hudson Taylor was Dr. Charles Gutzlaff, Secretary for
Chinese Affairs to the governor and government of Hong Kong. While
serving in his official role in Hong Kong, Gutzlaff sought to find
ways of evangelizing the Chinese. Out of daily prayer and Bible study
meetings in his government office, a new organization emerged with the
purpose of distributing and teaching the Scriptures in Mainland China.[9]

The work of Charles Gutzlaff attracted the interest of many in
Europe and led to the formation in 1850 of an association that became
known as the Chinese Evangelization Society (CES). Its purpose was the
spreading of the gospel in China through the combined efforts of foreign
missionaries and native evangelists. Although in time the CES became

---

[8]A. J. Broomhall, Hudson Taylor and China's Open Century:
Barbarians at the Gates, Book I (London: Hodder and Stoughton and
the Overseas Missionary Fellowship, 1981), p. 362

[9]Ibid., p. 28.

defunct, yet it was the vehicle God used to send Hudson Taylor as a young medical missionary to China in 1853 and thus launch a new movement.

Biographical Sketch of Hudson Taylor

Hudson Taylor was born at Barnsley, Yorkshire, England, in 1832. Even before his birth, Taylor's godly parents had prayed for a son who might become a missionary in China. Hudson's father was a pharmacist and a Methodist lay preacher, who had developed a burden for China through reading, especially the widely-circulated publication, China, written by Peter Parley.

Shortly after a conversion experience at age seventeen in 1849, Hudson Taylor came to the conviction that God was calling him to China as a missionary. Immediately Taylor began to prepare himself for that task in every way possible, including Chinese language study. Through reading Charles Medhurst's book, China, Taylor came to see the value of medical missions there, and in 1852 he began training in London Hospital to qualify as a doctor.

Earlier, Hudson Taylor had heard of the work of Charles Gutzlaff in China and began reading The Gleaner, published by the Chinese Association in London, which would soon become the Chinese Evangelization Society. However, in 1853, shortly before Taylor was to have completed his medical studies, significant political changes in China took place which seemed to indicate that Taylor should leave for China as quickly as possible. Terminating his medical studies, Taylor at the age of twenty sailed for the Middle Kingdom.

The next six years proved to be difficult. When Taylor arrived in China he soon discovered the administrative ineptitude of the CES, not to mention a wartorn country enveloped in the tragedy of a civil war known as the Taiping Rebellion, which over almost fifteen years' duration claimed over twenty million lives.[10] Only a handful of Protestant missionaries occupied the five treaty ports where they were allowed to operate. Christians numbered a meager 350 in all of the empire of China.[11]

The actions taken by the CES administration created frequent embarrassment and frustration, finally causing Taylor to resign in 1857. He continued working with former colleagues of the CES and others until health problems forced him to return to England in 1860. Even so, Taylor had already accomplished a great deal in China. He had taken several radical steps in adopting Chinese dress and lifestyle, along with trusting God alone for support. These ideas were developed further in the mission he would found in the future.

Formation of the China Inland Mission

In England Taylor reflected on the lessons learned during his first term of service in China. While recovering his health, Taylor felt constrained to do all in his power to mobilize others to take up the cause of China. He prayed earnestly for five missionaries to supplement the Ningpo mission, which Taylor had helped during his last two years in China. In addition, he spoke frequently at meetings, pressing home the urgent needs of China as well as visiting various denominational mission committees, hoping they would allocate further

---

[10]Broomhall, If I Had a Thousand Lives; Book III, p. 350.

[11]J. Hudson Taylor, China's Spiritual Need and Claims (London: Morgan and Scott, Ltd., 1887), p. 17.

resources and personnel to that field. Besides preaching and lecturing on China, Taylor completed his medical studies and also undertook, along with Frederick Gough of the Church Missionary Society, the revision of a colloquial version of the Ningpo New Testament. This project was to have a profound personal influence in preparing him for his future ministry.

By 1864, in spite of ongoing efforts to encourage other societies to action, Hudson Taylor was coming to the conviction that a new mission society was needed. He wrote in his Retrospect years later:

> Months of earnest prayer and not a few abortive efforts had resulted in a deep conviction that a special agency was essential for the evangelization of inland China. . . . The grave difficulty of possibly interfering with existing missionary operations at home was foreseen. . . .[12]

Thus, through six years of hard experiences in China and a further six years of prayer and reflection in England, the China Inland Mission (CIM), was formed in 1865.

In May 1866 Hudson Taylor with his wife and children, along with a party of sixteen missionaries, sailed for China. At that time there were some ninety-seven Protestant missionaries in the whole of China and only about 2,000 Christians. In eleven of the eighteen provinces there was not a single Protestant missionary. The goal of the CIM was to do widespread evangelism, and eventually to open up all the remaining eleven unoccupied provinces to the gospel. In due time Hudson Taylor's vision of reaching inland China was realized, and the small band which sailed in 1866 swelled to a mighty army of almost

---

[12]J. Hudson Taylor, A Retrospect (London: China Inland Mission. Agents: Religious Tract Society, 1900), p. 118.

1,400, becoming at one point the largest mission in the world.[13]

Principles and Practices of the CIM

In launching the CIM, Hudson Taylor created what he called "a special agency."[14] This new agency was needed, not only because of the disinterest or inability of others to expand their operations in China, but also in part because existing denominational societies were too tied to old methods and strategies. He envisioned an interdenominational mission made up of laymen and clergy, including women workers, with headquarters in China and dedicated to reaching particularly the inland provinces. The mission would have no fund-raising programs, but rather would look first to God and depend upon His faithfulness for its support.

The formation of the policies of the CIM covered a period of years, and many factors and individuals helped to shape its final form. Although the CIM was officially organized in 1865, yet the first statement of its principles and practices was not issued until 1875, when circumstances required further clarification of the structure, operations, and basic principles of the mission.

The principal distinctive features of the CIM were summarized later by Taylor as:

> First. Its interdenominational character.
> Second. That the workers have no guaranteed salary, but trust in God whom they serve to supply their needs, and are not disappointed in their trust.
> Third. That the direction of the work in the field is carried on, not by home committees, but by senior and experienced

---

[13]Stephen Neill, A History of Christian Missions (Harmondsworth, Middlesex, England: Penguin Books, Ltd., 1964), p. 333.

[14]Taylor, A Retrospect, p. 118.

missionaries, who help and guide as they are able those who have less experience in the Lord's work in China.

Fourth. That no personal solicitation or collection of funds is made, voluntary contributions alone being received, to which we may add that the mames of donors are never published, but each one receives a dated and numbered receipt by which he can trace his own contribution in the list of donations, and thence into the annually published accounts of the Mission.[15]

In addition, other major principles were clarified.

1. Membership was open to laymen and the less educated.

2. Missionary wives were considered missionaries in their own

   right and widespread use of single women workers was made.

3. Missionaries would wear Chinese dress, and as far as possible

   identify themselves with the Chinese people.

4. The primary aim of the Mission would be widespread evangelism,

   seeking to penetrate all of the unreached areas of China.

From our present perspective, the above principles do not appear unduly radical. Yet in the context of the time, Taylor and his Mission were in many ways out of step with other missions and churches of the Protestant world. Stephen Neill notes: "Many missionaries did not agree with Hudson Taylor's methods, regarding his work as dangerously superficial."[16]

Over the ensuing years, as the organization grew in complexity and encountered fresh problems, further refinements and additions were made to the original principles and practices. But the basic principles remained the same.

---

[15]Edwin Munsell Bliss, ed., The Encyclopedia of Missions (New York: Funk & Wagnalls, 1891), 2:1; 275.

[16]Neill, A History of Christian Missions, p. 336.

As the work expanded Taylor had to divide his time between home and field in giving direction. In 1872 a council of management was established in England to assist the ailing Home Director, Mr. W. T. Berger. The structure of the Mission began to assume the form it would retain until 1950. In 1873 Shanghai became the headquarters of the Mission, and from there the work was administrated.

The basic elements of the CIM's principles and practices had been forged in the crucible of hardship and firsthand experience while Taylor was in his first term of service in China between 1854-1860. His association with men like William Burns, the Scottish evangelist in China; John Burdon of the London Missionary Society; John Jones, and Dr. William Parker, Taylor's colleagues in Ningpo, all helped to crystallize what Taylor came to see as essential principles for spiritual ministry and effective missionary service.

From his return to England in 1860 to the actual formation of the CIM, again Taylor's thinking was considerably influenced by others such as George Muller, whose faith and prayer life served as an attractive model for the faith principles of the fledgling CIM. The itinerant evangelistic patterns of William Burns, and the strong commitment to lifestyle identification with the Chinese in clothing and manners that Charles Gutzlaff first demonstrated, also had a part in shaping the principles and policies which were woven into the CIM. The negative lessons learned through the administrative failures of the Chinese Evangelization Society probably enabled Taylor to formulate the new policies with a greater definitiveness and clarity than most of the later faith missions. Not only was the CIM born out of a sense of need, but also out of a reaction to a failure. From the beginning Taylor

sought to create a vehicle which would provide the greatest field

flexibility and facilitate the speediest possible evangelization of

China's millions. At the same time, the Principles and Practice of

the China Inland Mission stated clearly that:

> Every member of the Mission is expected to recognize
> that his dependence for the supply of all his need is on
> God, who called him and for whom he labors, and not on
> human organization.
> While candidates, therefore, when approved, may be
> assisted in their outfits for the voyage, may have their
> passage money paid for them, and may be supported in
> whole or in part by the funds of the Mission, their faith
> must be in God, their expectation from Him. The funds might
> fail, or the Mission might cease to exist, but if they
> put their trust in Him, He will never fail nor disappoint
> them. [17]

Many of the policies of the CIM were openly criticized by

others of the day, and even occasionally challenged from within. But

now Taylor's "special agency" was launched, and its distinctives and

principles would in time make a profound impact on the Christian world.

More attention will now be given to the various missiological dis-

tinctives of Hudson Taylor and the China Inland Mission.

---

[17]China Inland Mission, Instructions for Probationers and
Members of the CIM (Shanghai: China Inland Mission, 1925), p. 2.

CHAPTER II

PRIORITY OF THE UNREACHED

Statistics of China's population were more than of routine
interest to Hudson Taylor. From his conversion onward Taylor was made
aware through his father and others of the vast numbers of Chinese who
were still unreached with the gospel and the paucity of Christian missionaries in China. European churches were coming alive to the needs
of India and Africa, but by and large China had been neglected. In 1842
only six Protestant Chinese Christians were known in China. In 1853 the
total reached 350. By 1865 that figure had reached 2,000. In 1853
there were fifty-five Protestant missionaries to China, but by 1865 that
number had only risen to a total of ninety-seven.[1]

At the request of the editor of The Baptist Missionary Magazine
in December 1864, Taylor had begun to prepare a series of articles on
China. For four weeks Hudson Taylor compiled material, thought over the
subject, and then began to write. Mr. W. G. Lewis, editor of The Baptist
Missionary Magazine, recognized the importance of the articles and felt
strongly that they should have much wider circulation than his magazine
could provide. The content of those articles was expanded and carried over
into a booklet entitled China: Its Spiritual Need and Claims. Within this

_____

[1]Broomhall, If I Had a Thousand Lives, Book III, p. 363.

booklet Taylor's vision of the unreached millions in China and the biblical
need and responsibility of the church to systematically reach them came into
clear focus. The task ahead became evident, and from this point on
Taylor's ministry had a fresh sense of urgency and direction. All else
then became secondary to the one great purpose of taking the gospel of
Jesus Christ to those who had never heard in the land of China. The
specter of a million Chinese souls perishing without Christ each month
drove Taylor and the China Inland Mission to their knees and then to action.

Focus on the "Inland"

The very name of the mission Taylor had founded reflected his
burden for the millions who were unreached by the gospel. The
evangelization of inland China became the passion of his life, and all
his energies were concentrated to that end. Marshall Broomhall, Taylor's
nephew, described Taylor's focus:

> As a young man of twenty, we find Hudson Taylor writing to
> his mother: "I feel as if I could not live if something is not
> done for China. . . ." It is said of Cato that he closed every
> speech, no matter what its subject might be, with the words,
> "Carthage must be destroyed"; and with an infinitely higher aim,
> Hudson Taylor could not speak without including an appeal for
> the evangelization of China.[2]

Shortly after the formation of the CIM Taylor published
China's Spiritual Need and Claims. In this booklet the whole field
was carefully surveyed, with detail given to population figures, distribution of Christian workers and the status of each province throughout the
Chinese empire. Taylor showed that in each of the seven provinces

---

[2]Marshall Broomhall, Hudson Taylor: The Man Who Believed God,
seventh reprint (London: Overseas Missionary Fellowship, 1971), p. 204.

where Protestant work had commenced, there were still only ninety-one
workers seeking to reach 204 million Chinese within those provinces.
And beyond there were an additional eleven provinces in inland China, with
a population of 197 million for whom nothing had been attempted. After
setting forth the facts and figures of each province, the needs of the
outlying dependencies of China were also described.

Throughout the booklet the needs, possibilities and facilities
for reaching the inland provinces are all carefully reasoned. The
country was accessible to missionaries, Western churches had resources
and the Scriptures commanded the undertaking.

The first edition of this burning appeal in 1866 ran 3,000
copies, which were distributed and sold quickly. A second edition was
produced the following year, another in 1868, and a further edition in
1872. By 1877 the booklet had gone through seven editions and was
undoubtedly widely circulated with considerable impact.[3] Taylor
himself wrote in the preface of the seventh edition in reflection:

> Its circulation was blessed by God, and much interest in
> China was awakened. A number of persons were led to devote
> themselves to mission work there; some who joined the China
> Inland Mission, and some who are members of other missions,
> point to that book as having determined their course.[4]

A strong sense of priority for the unreached characterized
Taylor's thinking, speaking and writing over the years of his ministry.
This deep conviction of the plight of the lost helped to mold the
strategy of the CIM and compelled Taylor to urge other mission

---

[3]Marshall Broomhall, The Jubilee Story of the China Inland
Mission (Shanghai: China Inland Mission, 1915), pp. 27-28.

[4]Taylor, China's Spiritual Need and Claims, preface.

societies to take up the cause of the unreached as well.

Nor was Taylor's burden for the unreached limited to China.

Dr. Arthur Glasser in his foreword to the centennial issue of

J. Hudson Taylor: God's Man In China, notes:

> And yet those who knew Taylor intimately found that his
> heart extended far beyond China and the CIM. Dr. Harry Guinness,
> Director of the Regions Beyond Missionary Union, once recalled,
> 'I noticed that in his prayers he was always praying for South
> America. . . . His sympathies were as broad as the world, and
> it was South America every time he prayed.' As a missionary
> speaker he never pleaded for the CIM. The claims of the whole
> world were ever before him; they were the substance of his
> ministry. A friend commented: 'It was just as much joy to him
> when men went to Africa or to Japan. . . as it was when they
> went to China. . . . It was the world that he wanted for Christ.[5]

Not only the map but also the Bible impelled Hudson Taylor to

focus on the "inlands" of China and to seek to proclaim the gospel

there. For Taylor the sense of obligation and obedience to the command

of Christ, coupled with a sense of the tragic plight of the lost, were

fundamental motivations. In the 1877 edition of China's Spiritual Need

and Claims Taylor demonstrates his spiritual motivation in missions when

he says:

> My reader, think of the over 80 millions beyond the reach
> of the gospel in the seven provinces where missionaries have
> longest labored; think of the over 100 millions in the other
> eleven provinces of China proper, beyond the reach of the few
> missionaries laboring there; think of the over 20 millions
> who inhabit the vast regions of Manchuria, Mongolia, Tibet,
> and the Northwestern dependencies, which exceed in extent the
> whole of Europe--an aggregate of over 200 millions beyond the
> reach of all existing agencies--and how shall

> > God's name be hallowed by them,
> > His Kingdom come among them, and
> > His will be done by them?

---

[5]Arthur F. Glasser, Foreword to J. Hudson Taylor: God's Man in
China by Dr. and Mrs. Howard Taylor (Chicago: Moody Press, 1965), p. vi.

His name, His attributes they have never heard. His kingdom is not proclaimed among them. His will is not made known to them. Do you <u>believe</u> that each unit of these millions has a precious soul and that "there is none other name under heaven given amongst men whereby they must be saved" than that of Jesus? Do you believe that He alone is "the Door of the sheepfold"; is "the Way, the Truth, and the Life?" And that "no man cometh unto the Father but by Him"? If so, think of the state of these unsaved ones; and solemnly examine yourself in the sight of God to see whether you are doing your utmost to make Him known to them.[6]

Over ten years later in 1889, Taylor published another leaflet and corresponding article in China's Millions which also had a considerable impact in focusing attention on the unreached and the inlands of China. The leaflet entitled To Every Creature deals again with the problem and practicability of evangelizing China. Taylor pointed out that with a thousand additional evangelists there was every possibility of adequately reaching all of China. This in turn became the basis of a wide interdenominational appeal and prayer target of 1,000 new missionaries for China.

Underlying the To Every Creature appeal was the deep theological conviction of the lostness of man, the validity of the Great Commission, and the church's solemn responsibility to obey. With carefully chosen words Taylor implored:

How are we going to treat the Lord Jesus Christ in reference to this command? Shall we definitely drop the title Lord as applied to Him, and take the ground that we are quite willing to recognize Him as Saviour Jesus, so far as the eternal penalty of sin is concerned, but are not prepared to recognize ourselves as bought with a price, or Him as having any claim to our unquestioning obedience? Shall we say that we are our own masters, willing to recognize something as His due, who bought us with His blood, provided He does not ask too much: our lives, our loved ones, our possessions are our own, not His; we will give Him what we think fit, and obey any of His commands that do not demand too great a sacrifice? To be taken to heaven by Jesus Christ we are

---

[6]Taylor, <u>China's Spiritual Need and Claims</u>, p. 39.

more than willing, but we will not have this man to reign over us.[7]

Not a mere human project but a divine command was what Taylor saw in the words "to every creature." It was a question of duty to reach the unreached of China, and no time could be lost. "'If we begin at once,' he realized afresh with a straitened heart, 'millions will have passed away ere we can reach them.'"[8]

Evangelistic Strategy

Growing out of Hudson Taylor's priority of the unreached was an innovative but highly criticized evangelistic strategy. This strategy had a number of implications for the kinds of missionaries recruited as well as their deployment and affected the course of overall missions in China.

In referring to Taylor's evangelistic strategy, Latourette said:

> The main purpose of the CIM was not to win converts or to build a Chinese church, but to spread a knowledge of the Christian Gospel throughout the empire as quickly as might be. . . . The purpose was to cover the entire empire so far as that was untouched by other Protestant agencies. Once the Christian message had been proclaimed, the fruits in conversions might be gathered by others. The aim was the presentation of the Christian message throughout the empire in the shortest possible time, not the immediate winning of the largest numbers of converts. In accord with this programme, the China Inland Mission did not seek primarily to build churches, although these were gathered. Nor, although Chinese assistants were employed, did it stress the recruiting and training of Chinese ministry.[9]

---

[7]China's Millions, 1889:172-73.

[8]Taylor, God's Man in China, p. 312

[9]K. S. Latourette, A History of the Expansion of Christianity (New York: MacMillan Co., 1929), 6:329.

Taylor's emphasis from the beginning was outreach by itineration with localized, settled work following behind. In this strategy he had drawn from others before, particularly from men like Gutzlaff and his close friend, William Burns. Hudson Taylor summarized the evolution of his evangelistic strategy in the following way:

> The relation of itinerant to settled missionary work is a subject in which I have long taken the deepest interest. It was first suggested to me in 1848 by the publication of the accounts of Gutzlaff's Missionary Union by Secretaries of the Chinese Evangelisation Society. This Society, which sent me out to China in 1853 had, from the commencement, strongly advocated the fullest development of itinerant work. The early itinerations in China of Medhurst, Milne and Edkins of the London Missionary Society, and yet more especially of my revered friend, the late Rev. William Burns--with whom I personally itinerated in 1855-56 in Kiangsu, Chehkiang, and the Swatow district of Kwangtung--gradually deepened my interest in the subject, and my sense of its importance. Indeed, the views impressed upon me by Mr. Burns, who had labored as an evangelist in Scotland, England and Canada before going out, and whose life in China had been that of an itinerant evangelist, have molded the whole of my subsequent life, and been largely influential in the formation and course of the China Inland Mission.[10]

In spite of sharp criticism from other groups, Taylor's evangelistic strategy, in his own mind at least, was based on careful reasoning and followed a systematic plan. Itineration trips, rather than being "aimless wanderings" or "frantic evangelization" were intended to be initial steps in the ultimate establishment of the church in China. His plan of operation was outlined carefully as recorded in an article in the first editions of China's Millions in 1875:

> The study of the Acts of the Apostles leads to the conclusion that a plan of missionary operations, somewhat like that adopted by them, would prove the most effective wherever the needy territories are large and the laborers are few. In China we might mass our missionaries at the Free Ports; but such stations

---

[10] James Johnston, ed., Report of the Centenary Conference on Protestant Missions of the World, London, 1888 (New York: Fleming H. Revell, 1888), 2:29.

while convenient for correspondence and European society, would
have the disadvantages of all the evil influences of a large
and nominally Christian community, among whom are many whose
lives are less moral than those of the heathen around them.
The early missionaries appear rather to have scattered themselves. They visited important centres, usually in twos or
threes, stayed long enough to commence a work, and then trusted
much to the keeping of God, and to such help as could be afforded
by epistles and occasional visits for its further progress. They
had advantages which we do not possess in China, in the godly Jews
and proselytes already acquainted with the Old Testament Scriptures,
who were found everywhere and who, when converted soon became able
to lead and instruct the converts from among the heathen. We
may, therefore, anticipate the necessity of a somewhat prolonged
residence in our districts for the purpose of instructing in the
Word of God those who may be converted. Still, the general principle,
if a true one, should be kept in mind. Our desire, therefore, is:

First, to send two missionaries together with two native
converts, to each unevangelized province of China, who may
begin by itinerating through the province and gather believers
as the Lord enables them; locating themselves for a period of
years in some important centre (say, the capital of the
province if practicable), when He gives an open door.
Next, with the aid of converted natives of the province,
to extend the work to the capitals of the circuits, then to
prefectures, and subsequently to the country cities, from
which it may easily be carried to the more important towns and
villages of the country itself.[11]

From the beginning, as defined in the Principles and Practice,

the aim of the CIM was: "By the help of God to bring the Chinese to a

saving knowledge of the love of Christ by means of itinerant and

localized work throughout the whole of the interior of China."[12]

Taylor's policy was to see an opening in the capital of the province,

even though it was recognized as a difficult place in which to gather

a church. The next step was to open stations in the prefectures;

then in subordinate cities. The chief reason for this procedure was

---

[11]China's Millions, 1875–76:31.

[12]China Inland Mission, Probationers and Members of the CIM,
p. 2.

that subordinate officials were more likely to allow missionary activity

if higher officials had approved, and it was also anticipated that with

churches established in the cities, the villages thus would be more

easily influenced.[13]

Taylor frequently had to justify his actions to others, however,

and at times the whole issue became the subject of heated debate. Behind

his reasoning, however, was the strong conviction that the primary aim

of missions was the evangelization and not the Christianization of China.

Furthermore, Taylor felt that itinerant evangelism should not be pitted

against localized work as both were important. In a prepared study paper

on missionary methods given at the Missionary Conference in London, 1888,

Taylor stressed:

> To prevent misconception, it may be well at the very outset
> to notice that our subject is the relation of itinerant to
> settled missionary work; it is not itinerant versus settled
> missionary work. Both are essential and important, and so far
> from being antagonistic are mutually dependent upon each other.[14]

He went on to explain that in the early stages itineration was necessary

because of the difficulty of settling due to local opposition or

hostility:

> We attempted twenty-two years ago without previous itineration
> to open stations as convenient centres for future evangelistic
> work; but these efforts frequently resulted in opposition, or
> even riots, arising from the superstitious fears of the people
> and the hostility of the literati. We then reversed the process,
> notwithstanding that it involved much difficulty and labor. We
> first itinerated through large and remote districts, and seeking
> the guidance of God, selected suitable points for future head-
> quarters. These places were visited frequently, friends were made,
> and we became well-known before attempting a settlement, which then

---

[13]China's Millions, 1875-76:31

[14]Johnston, ed., Report of the Missionary Conference, London,
1888, 2:29.

was accomplished with little difficulty, and without subsequent
cause for regret. The stations thus ·formed were both the outcome of preliminary itinerations and the prelude to more
thorough and systematic work in the provinces in question.[15]

Hudson Taylor in historical perspective has been criticized as
having a low view of the church and neglecting church growth for aggressive
evangelism. And yet a careful reading of the historical documents will
show clearly that Taylor's goal in evangelism was the establishing of
local churches. In fact, A. J. Broomhall records that the very first
missionary efforts of the China Inland Mission resulted in a strong, virile
church in Ningpo.[16] Furthermore, the accounts of the earliest activities
of the CIM between 1865-1875, as detailed in the Occasional Papers, are
full of references to church nurture, discipling, and training of church
leadership. By 1890 the Mission, in addition to penetrating the majority
of the heretofore unreached inland provinces, had established some 150
stations and substations, with eighty organized churches and baptized
converts numbering approximately 3,000. Ten years later the number of
baptisms would swell to almost 13,000.[17]

It is true, however, that evangelism and the priority of the
unreached were the overriding motivational factors in the CIM. In the
early stages long itinerations were taken, which may have been ques-
tionable in terms of productivity. In defense of this evangelistic
strategy Alexander Wylie of the London Missionary Society wrote, "They

---

[15]Ibid., p. 30.

[16]Broomhall, If I Had a Thousand Lives, Book III, p. 441.

[17]China's Millions, 1890:101-02.

are opening up the country and this is what we want. Their missionaries
are doing a good work."[18] Furthermore, a British Consul remarked in his
official report to Parliament in 1880:

> Always on the move, the missionaries of this society have
> traveled throughout the country, taking hardship and privation
> as the natural incidents of their profession, and never attempting
> to force themselves anywhere, they have made friends everywhere;
> and, while laboring in their special field as ministers of the
> Gospel, have accustomed the Chinese to the presence of foreigners
> among them, and in great measure dispelled the fear of the
> barbarian, which has been the main difficulty with which we have
> had to contend.[19]

Institutional work, as mentioned earlier, was adjunct, although
in time it grew in importance. The CIM devoted considerable efforts and
resources to education, medical work, literature production and literacy,
along with relief and development efforts. In a Ph.D. dissertation on
the CIM in the area of institutional work, Dr. H. T. Armerding documented
the considerable contribution made by CIM particularly in the inland
areas of China, which served both as an aid to evangelism and a
service to the nation.[20]

Recruitment Appeals

Always for Hudson Taylor the priority of the lost determined the
ultimate strategy of the work. As a result, his eyes were constantly on
the unreached inlands and appeals were directed to recruitment of those
who could possibly reach them:

---

[18]Dr. and Mrs. Howard Taylor, Hudson Taylor and the China
Inland Mission: The Growth of a Work of God (London: China Inland
Mission, 1918), p. 350.

[19]Ibid., p. 350.

[20]Hudson Taylor Armerding, "China Inland Mission and Some Aspects
of its Work" (Ph.D dissertation, University of Chicago, 1948).

Oh that the Spirit might be so poured out from on high that
from our home pulpits many ministers might be constrained to leave
their surfeited congregations; that in the foreign field many missionaries might be impelled to leave to the care of resident natives,
schools, and chapels, among those who have already heard the
Gospel, alike to emphasise by obedience the reality of the Gospel
and preach it everywhere until not an unevangelized village remains!
It is not sufficient to be doing a work good in itself, while the
Master's great commission is unfulfilled; and that commission is to
"Preach the Gospel to every creature." And yet we all know that
three-quarters of the world's population have never had it offered
to them! What Christ commanded eighteen hundred years ago, and
what the needs of the world now demand is itinerant work. The unevangelized now living have but a few years to live; and the
immediate and urgent necessity of the world is earnest, widespread
itinerant evangelization.[21]

In the modern history of the missionary movement Hudson Taylor
and the CIM are unique in the special appeals that were made for new
workers and the way in which those workers appeared. The various appeals
over the years captured the attention of many, and in turn became incentive
to others and a real stimulus to faith.

The first appeal for workers for the CIM came on June 25, 1865,
as Hudson Taylor committed himself to the formation of the Mission during
the famous Brighton Beach incident. Although Taylor had already prayed
for five new reinforcements for the Ningpo Mission, yet the appeal for
the twenty-four was a bold new step.

On Sunday, June 25th, 1865, unable to bear the sight of a
congregation of a thousand or more Christian people rejoicing
in their own security, while millions were perishing for lack of
knowledge, I wandered out on the sands alone, in great spiritual
agony; and there the Lord conquered my unbelief, and I surrendered
myself to God for this service. I told Him that all the responsibility as to issues and consequences must rest with Him; that as
His servant it was mine to obey and to follow Him--His to direct,
to care for, and to guide me and those who might labor with me.
Need I say that peace at once flowed into my burdened heart? There
and then I asked Him for twenty-four fellow workers, two for each
of the eleven inland provinces which were without a missionary, and

---

[21]Johnston, ed., Report of the Missionary Conference, London,
1888, 2:31,32.

two for Mongolia; and writing the petition on the margin of the Bible
I had with me, I returned home with a heart enjoying rest such as
it had been a stranger to for months, and with an assurance that the
Lord would bless His own work and that I should share in the blessing.[22]

By the close of 1866, the above appeal was fully answered, and a
total of twenty-eight workers made up the still-fledgling CIM. Over
the next several years a small but steady stream of reinforcements joined
the CIM.

A survey of the early development of the CIM reveals periodic
calls for advance, usually tied to a call for a stated number of new
workers. Frequently the calls came at times when conditions in China
were least propitious for advance. Human wisdom would have sounded a
retreat, but confidence in the faithfulness and power of God coupled
with a deep burden for the unreached prompted Taylor and his fellow
workers to call for additional workers.

The first call for advance came in 1875. Mission funds were
at an exceedingly low point, and even Taylor himself had been bedridden
due to a back injury suffered in a fall. However, the specter of nine
provinces--each the size of a European country averaging a population
of seventeen million--drove Taylor to appeal in faith. In the issue of
The Christian for January 21, 1875, there appeared "an appeal for prayer"
in which Taylor pleaded in behalf of more than 150 million unreached
Chinese. He concluded by urging ". . . Will each of your readers at once
raise his heart to God and wait one minute in earnest prayer that God will
raise up this year eighteen suitable men to devote themselves to this
work. . . ?"[23] In response to the challenge for eighteen men, sixty
offered! Ten were accepted and sailed in 1875, with eight more following

---

[22]Taylor, A Retrospect, pp. 119-120.

[23]Leslie T. Lyall, A Passion for the Impossible, second ed.
(London: Overseas Missionary Fellowship, 1976), p. 43.

the next year.

A second call for advance came in 1881. With a total number of CIM missionaries still numbering barely a hundred, a small group of senior CIM missionaries gathered for a week of prayer and consultation with Hudson Taylor in Wuchang. Recent surveys had indicated many open doors and great needs for evangelistic expansion. With a strong sense of conviction, based on assessed needs, the band prayed for forty-two men and twenty-eight women--or seventy workers in all--to be given by 1884. An appeal was drafted and signed by seventy-seven members of the Mission and published finally in China's Millions for February 1883.[24]

The response was overwhelming. Offers of service came from many, and by 1884 seventy-three new workers had sailed for China. They in turn were followed shortly by the famous Cambridge Seven, whose response and dedication to missionary work in China stirred the church at home, which in turn sparked additional offers of service.

A third major advance came in 1886, when another significant appeal for workers was made. Based on a careful survey of needs, the newly formed China Council of the CIM cabled home in December 1886 the following message: "Banded prayer next year 100 new workers. Send soon as possible."[25] At least one hundred new workers were clearly needed if progress already made was to be consolidated, strong churches established, and new outreach initiated. The prayer for The Hundred was amazingly answered by the end of 1887, when 102 were on their way out to China out of a total of 600 who offered!

---

[24]China's Millions, February 1883: 13-17

[25]Lyall, A Passion for the Impossible, 58-59.

But the vision of Hudson Taylor was far from dead. In 1889 he wrote a paper entitled "To Every Creature" in which a plan was outlined for realizing the passion of his life--the total evangelization of China. The paper was prepared for the 1890 Missionary Conference in Shanghai, when 400 delegates from forty societies were to meet. In Hudson Taylor's opening message to the conference he appealed for a thousand new workers to reach the whole of China.

The appeal for The Thousand met with warm response, and between October 1890 and March 1891, CIM alone received no fewer than 126 new workers. Five years after the appeal for The Thousand it was estimated that 1,153 new workers had arrived in China under all missions.[26]

In the years that followed, the work of the CIM made other significant advances and other appeals were issued, including the famous appeal for the Two Hundred in 1929. But each appeal was based on the assumption that advance was mandatory, and no efforts must be spared in reaching the unreached.

---

[26]Ibid., p. 61.

CHAPTER III

MOVING MEN BY PRAYER ALONE

To many Christians the name of Hudson Taylor is almost synonymous with faith and finance. Perhaps more than any other distinctive, Taylor's convictions on mission finance and the record of God's supply for him and the CIM have attracted the notice and admiration of the Christian public. Hudson Taylor was convinced that God's work done in God's way would never lack God's supply.[1] Without promise of aid from any church or institution Taylor took the first band of CIMers to China in 1866, and without appeals for support he saw God's faithful provision for the Mission never fail over the next forty years.

For Taylor the matter of finances was no side issue. God's command to go was also seen as God's promise to provide. Taylor's view on mission finance held considerable missiological implications and affected important areas such as recruitment, work strategy and church-mission relations. Confidence in God's ability to supply all the needs of His children involved in doing His work became a characteristic of Hudson Taylor and served frequently as a stimulus to faith on the part of many others. In fact, in this regard Taylor and the CIM perhaps have fulfilled one of their most

---

[1]Frank Houghton, comp., The Fire Burns On: CIM Anthology 1865-1965 (London: Overseas Missionary Fellowship, 1965), p. 93.

significant roles. As Dr. S. D. Gordon put it, "I have a very strong feeling that God means to use and is using the missionaries of the CIM far more than a service to China."[2]

Taylor's financial policies were forged out of the crucible of experience, both prior to and after becoming a missionary to China. In 1887, when the CIM was twenty-two years old, Taylor looked back and related the faithfulness of God's provision in answer to prayer alone:

> Those who have never been called to prove the faithfulness
> of the covenant-keeping God, in supplying in answer to prayer
> the pecuniary need of His servants, might deem it a hazardous
> experiment to send evangelists to a distant heathen land with
> "only God to look to." But in one whose privilege it has been
> for many years past to prove the faithfulness of God in various
> circumstances--at home and abroad, by land and by sea, in sickness
> and in health, in necessities, in dangers, and at the gates of
> death--such apprehensions would be wholly inexcusable. The writer
> has seen God, in answer to prayer, quell the raging storm, alter
> the direction of the wind, and give rain in the midst of prolonged
> drought. He has seen Him, in answer to prayer, stay the angry
> passions and murderous intentions of violent men, and bring the
> machinations of His people's foes to nought. He has seen Him, in
> answer to prayer, raise the dying from the bed of death, when human
> aid was vain; has seen Him preserve from the pestilence that
> walketh in darkness, and from the destruction that wasteth at
> noonday. For more than twenty-seven years he has proved the faith-
> fulness of God in supplying pecuniary means for his own temporal
> wants and for the need of the work he has been engaged in. He has
> seen God, in answer to prayer, raising up laborers not a few for
> this vast mission field; supplying the means requisite for their
> outfit, passage, and support; vouchsafing blessing on the efforts
> of many of them, both among the native Christians and the heathen
> Chinese in fourteen out of the eighteen provinces referred to.[3]

Nonsolicitation for Finance

Fundamental to the principles and practices of the CIM was the policy of nonsolicitation and nonindebtedness. Having suffered considerably under the financial ineptitude of the Chinese Evangelization

---

[2]Ibid., p. 97.

[3]Taylor, China's Spiritual Need and Claims, p. 49.

Society and the subsequent embarrassment, Hudson Taylor committed himself

as early as 1857 to live in dependence upon God alone and not to appeal

for support. This conviction carried over into the policies of the CIM,

and is reflected in the same way today in the successor to the CIM, the

Overseas Missionary Fellowship. The financial policy of the Mission is

stated in the following terms:

> The Fellowship is supported by God, normally through the
> freewill offerings of God's people. The needs of the work
> are laid before God in prayer, and no member of the Fellowship
> is authorized to solicit funds on his own behalf or that of the
> Fellowship, and no announcement of material needs is authorized.
> This does not preclude a frank answer being made to an inquiry
> or the acceptance of an offering at meetings arranged by others
> and taken up on their initiative. The membership agrees that,
> for them, going into debt would be inconsistent with their
> principle of entire dependence upon God.[4]

The basis for the nonsolicitation policy is derived primarily from

Taylor's understanding of Scripture and the pattern of God's work. He wrote:

> Are we not told to seek first the kingdom of God--not means to
> advance it--and that all these things shall be added to us? Such
> promises are surely sufficient. I saw that the Apostolic plan was
> not to raise ways and means, but to go and do the work, trusting in
> His promises who said: "Seek first the kingdom of God and His
> righteousness and all these things shall be added unto you."[5]

In other words, Hudson Taylor saw his responsibility to obey and

do the work and God's responsibility was to supply the needs. In an oft-

quoted statement the missionary pioneer summarized this basic financial

principle on the twenty-first anniversary of the CIM:

---

[4]Overseas Missionary Fellowship, Principles and Practice
(Singapore: Overseas Missionary Fellowship, 1968), p. 7.

[5]Marshall Broomhall, Our Seal (London: The China Inland
Mission, 1933), p. 11.

Our Father is a very experienced One: He knows very well
that His children wake up with a good appetite every morning,
and He always provides breakfast for them; and He does not send
His children supperless to bed at night. "Bread shall be
given. . . waters shall be sure." He sustained three millions
of Israelites in the wilderness for forty years. We do not
expect that He will send three million missionaries to China, but if
He did, He would have plenty of means to sustain them all. Let
us see that we keep God before our eyes; that we walk in His
ways and seek to please and glorify Him in everything great and
small. Depend upon it. God's work done in God's way will never
lack God's supplies.[6]

To Taylor personally it seemed inconsistent to trust God and yet

appeal for funds. He once wrote to a Council member, "I do beg that never

any appeal for funds be put forward, save to God in prayer. When our work

becomes a begging work, it dies. God is faithful, must be so."[7] And again

Taylor clarified this fundamental financial principle when he said in an

address to fellow CIM missionaries: "I do want you to realize this principle

of working with God, and asking Him for everything. If the work is at the

command of God, then we can go to Him. . . for the means."[8]

Competition Avoidance

Hudson Taylor's policy was based not only on his understanding of

biblical principles but also came out of a specific historical context.

At the time of the formation of the China Inland Mission in 1865, inter-

denominational organizations were virtually nonexistent. It is true,

however, that the great evangelical revival that had swept across

denominational lines had helped to create greater toleration and fellowship

---

[6]Houghton, The Fire Burns On, p. 93.

[7]Taylor, God's Man in China, p. 238.

[8]Houghton, The Fire Burns On, p. 92.

among groups. In fact, some undenominational congregations were springing up in England at that time, thus contributing to a better understanding of a mission like the CIM. Still denominational mission programs were the norm of the day.[9]

As Taylor moved around England in 1865-66 seeking to challenge the church to its responsibilities towards China, he became concerned that in forming the CIM he might divert interest and gifts from existing channels. Taylor felt that every effort on behalf of China and other non-Christian lands was more than needed, and he was fearful that the newly-born CIM might become a hindrance. To avoid deflecting monies from denominational channels, Taylor adopted the nonsolicitation policy.

At the same time, Taylor never attacked or criticized the financial principles of other missions or claimed that the policies adopted by the CIM were necessarily better--or even more biblical. They implied no criticism of the general practices of the older societies, and Taylor was extremely concerned that support should not be diverted from them to the CIM. He tried to make this more difficult by refusing to authorize offerings when he himself or his colleagues were invited to speak at various denominational churches. But while making no special claims for these practices, Taylor firmly believed that the methods adopted were the God-given pattern for the CIM. He felt that God had raised up the CIM to become a monument to one thing: the utter faithfulness of God and the practicalness of a simple trust in God as a basis for living.[10]

---

[9]Broomhall, If I Had a Thousand Lives, Book III, p. 389.

[10]Lyall, A Passion for the Impossible, Second ed., p. 38.

Nonindebtedness

Growing out of a policy of nonsolicitation was a related principle
of nonindebtedness. Going into debt seemed to Hudson Taylor a violation
of God's pattern for work, and also a negative reflection upon the
faithfulness of God. Again, Taylor's own unhappy experience with the CES
and its frequent indebtedness colored his thinking considerably and moved
him to this policy.

To Hudson Taylor nonindebtedness was a close corollary of trusting
God alone for finances. He once remarked on this theme:

> It is really just as easy for God to give beforehand; and
> He much prefers to do so. He is too wise to allow His purposes
> to be frustrated for lack of a little money; but money wrongly
> placed or obtained in unscriptural ways is sure to hinder
> blessing.
> And what does going into debt really mean? It means that
> God has not supplied your need. You trusted Him, but He has
> not given you the money; so you supply yourself and borrow. If
> we can only wait right up to the time, God cannot lie, God cannot
> forget; He is pledged to supply all our need.[11]

In other words, human planning must be secondary to recognizing
the will of God, and action must follow provision of the means. Thus
God's guidance was very clearly linked to God's timing of provision, and
the withholding of provision was taken as God's leading to wait or move
in a different direction. Thus Taylor would not commit the Mission to a
program which would necessitate going into debt.

At the same time new workers were never held back from going to
the field until support funds were in hand. Each missionary was expected
to look to God alone for support, and to contribute his share of faith
to the pooling system which the Mission adopted. It is an amazing record

---

[11]Taylor, The Growth of a Work of God, p. 54.

indeed to see over the years how, even in spite of heavy and rapid increases in personnel, Mission funds increased commensurately and the work on the field continued.

An interesting illustration of this can be found in the appeal for The Seventy in 1881. Taylor and his fellow workers, after a careful survey, concluded that seventy new workers were required, and so gave themselves to pray for the seventy, along with large reinforcements for all the other societies working in China. At the same time, however, Mission funds were low, and nothing in hand was available to provide for the expected influx. No sooner had the appeal for seventy appeared in the China's Millions in 1883 than an unexpected large gift on behalf of a whole family arrived to cover all the necessary outgoing expenses. Income thereafter also continued to keep pace with the increased number of workers.

Dedicated Gifts and Donors

Hudson Taylor's policy of nonsolicitation was influenced in part by another important consideration. He was deeply concerned for the spiritual welfare of each donor along with the church at home, and he felt that appeals or pressure tactics to give in meetings might undercut the true work God was seeking to do. In other words, collections taken at meetings might incite people to respond emotionally; whereas, God might be asking for more than a few dollars given on the spot.

This is illustrated in a particular instance that took place in 1866, shortly before the first CIM party sailed for China. Following the close of a message by Hudson Taylor, the chairman of the meeting announced that although no offering had been planned, yet he felt it would be appropriate. The chairman sensed that many present would be distressed and burdened if deprived of the opportunity to contribute towards Mr. Taylor's work, and so set about to take up a collection. At that point Hudson Taylor intervened and asked permission to explain. His remarks reveal Taylor's convictions. He expressed his desire that his hearers should go away burdened. However, money was not the chief thing in the Lord's work, especially money easily given under the influence of emotion. As much as he appreciated their kind intention, he would far rather have each one go home and ask the Lord very definitely what He would have them do. If it were to give of their substance they could send a contribution to some missionary society. But he added that God might be asking much more in the light of the appalling needs of the mission field, perhaps even a son or daughter, or one's own life for missionary service.

After the meeting the host expressed disappointment to Taylor for stopping the collections. In spite of further explanations, the gentleman remained unconvinced. Next morning at breakfast, however, the host appeared and confessed a remarkable change in attitude:

> I felt last evening that you were wrong about the collection, but now I see things differently. Lying awake in the night, as I thought of that stream of souls in China, a thousand every hour going out into the dark, I could only cry, 'Lord what wilt Thou have me to do?' If there had been a collection I should have given a five pound note. This cheque is the result of no small part of the night spent in prayer.[12]

The check was for 500 pounds sterling and just covered the passage fares for the China party. Hudson Taylor felt keenly that no amount of money could save a single soul. He preferred to see people giving themselves first to prayer and then to the work in China, being convinced that funds would never be lacking for God-sent missionaries. Taylor summarized his feelings when he said:

---

[12]Taylor, God's Man in China, p. 180.

If our hearts are right we may count upon the Holy Spirit's
working through us to bring others into deeper fellowship with
God--the way the work began at Pentecost. We do not need to say
much about the CIM. Let people see God working, let God be
glorified, let believers be made holier, happier, brought nearer
to Him, and they will not need to be asked to help.[13]

On another occasion Taylor emphasized his convictions on

support and missions:

Money wrongly placed and money given from wrong motives
are both to be greatly dreaded. We can afford to have as
little as the Lord chooses to give, but we cannot afford to
have unconsecrated money, or to have money placed in the
wrong position. Far better have no money at all, even to
buy food with; for there are plenty of ravens in China, and
the Lord could send them again with bread and flesh.[14]

The policy of nonsolicitation then was to encourage in part the

giving of dedicated gifts from dedicated donors. Taylor also saw it as a

way to liberate the missionary from anxiety regarding the financial

outcome of meetings and services. As Taylor described it: "The missionary

is then free in spirit, occupied with God rather than man, and more eager

to give than to get."[15]

God's Faithfulness

Punctuating the writings and messages of Hudson Taylor are

innumerable references to the faithfulness of God. For Taylor this theme

was central to his life and became a frequent point of comment. The Mis-

sion's financial policy related to this theological truth as well. Even

the CIM slogan or watchword--Ebenezer ("Hitherto hath the Lord helped us")

and Jehovah Jireh ("The Lord will provide") reflected the reality of the

faithfulness of God.

---

[13]Ibid., pp. 175-176.   [14]Ibid., p. 171.

[15]Houghton, The Fire Burns On, p. 109.

And yet the historical record shows that there were many times of financial stringency. Often faith was tested to the limit during periods of low income. Several critical points were reached just before The Seventy went out in 1882, and again in 1887 prior to The Hundred. But each period of shortfall was seen as a trial of faith and not a failure on God's part to provide. In contemplating the need for additional workers, Taylor reflected his confidence in God when he said:

> Not to advance would be to retreat from the position of
> faith taken up at the beginning. It would be to look at
> difficulties rather than at the living God. True, funds were low--
> had been for years, and the workers coming out from home few,
> while several retirements had taken place in China. Difficulties
> were formidable; and it was easy to say, 'All these things are
> indications that for the present no further extension is possible.'
> But not to go forward would be to throw away opportunities God had
> given.[16]

When income would drop, Hudson Taylor would search his own life again, prayerfully considering every aspect of the work to see if there might be anything hindering the blessing of the Lord in this respect. A strong sense of stewardship gripped Taylor, believing that every gift to the Mission was the outcome of a divinely-given impulse.

At times of testing Taylor would come back, however, to the fundamental conviction that God had called the CIM into being, and it was God's responsibility to maintain it. "Have faith in God" became a recurring note in Taylor's messages, or as he translated Mark 11:22, "Hold the faithfulness of God." In an article written for China's Millions in 1875, the implications of the faithfulness of God were summarized:

> Holding His faithfulness, we may go into every province of
> China. Holding His faithfulness, we may face, with calm and
> sober but confident assurance of victory, every difficulty and
> danger. We may count on grace for the work, on pecuniary aid,

---

[16]Taylor, God's Man in China, p. 270.

on needful facilities, and on ultimate success. Let us not give Him a partial trust, but daily, hourly serve Him, holding God's faithfulness.[17]

Pooling Support System

In the "special agency" designed by Hudson Taylor, funds received were to be shared equally among the members. This unique pooling system was seen as an expression of the family spirit of the CIM and their mutual dependence upon God.

Taylor made it clear to each candidate from the beginning that the Mission could not guarantee his or her support, nor assure a regular salary. The CIM did not send missionaries to China as paid agents. Rather, the Mission would only send

> . . . men who believe that God has called them to the work, who go there to labour for God, and can therefore trust Him, whose they are and whom they serve, to supply their temporal needs. We gladly cooperate with--providing if needful, outfit and passage money, and such a measure of support as circumstances call for and we are enabled to supply. Our faith is sometimes tried, but God always proves Himself faithful, and at the right time supplies all our needs.[18]

The pooling system didn't limit personal gifts from other sources reaching individual missionaries. Frequently, personally designated gifts were seen as God's special provision for needs not met through the normal shared Mission funds. But in the end each member was cast upon God, who would never fail him.

-----

[17]China's Millions, 1875: 55.

[18]Taylor, God's Man in China, p. 242.

CHAPTER IV

IDENTIFICATION

In the past decade contextualization has become a hot topic in
mission circles, much as the term indigenization was a few years earlier.
Cross-cultural communication of the gospel and the form of a national
church are crucial matters, and missionaries over the years have wrestled
with the issues involved.

Over a century ago in China Hudson Taylor came to grips early
in his ministry with the challenges of indigenization and contextualization without knowing the modern labels. Taylor's perception of
cultural barriers to the communication of the gospel and the expansion
of the church in China led him to adopt a radical approach in mission
methodology.

Taylor's first major step in seeking to identify more closely
with the Chinese was to adapt his clothing and appearance. His adoption of Chinese dress and customs grew in time to wider implications
for his ministry and developed also into a distinct set of policies
for the CIM. Although Hudson Taylor was not totally unique in his
efforts to identify with the Chinese, yet his attempts at cultural
accommodation were innovative and became a model and stimulus for
others.

A Chinese to the Chinese

The image of a Westerner in China in the mid-nineteenth century was far from a pleasant one. Contact with foreigners over the years had frequently been under adverse circumstances. In particular, the incessant efforts of the Western Powers to force their commercial demands on a sovereign China were seen as despicable. For centuries the Chinese had viewed themselves as the Middle Kingdom, and in fact the center of the civilized world. Foreigners had basically only brought trouble and grief to China and were looked down upon as barbarians and devils. At best the handful of Westerners residing in China in the 1850s were tolerated by the Chinese, and at worst they were despised, feared and hated.

Thus when Hudson Taylor first reached China in 1854, he encountered tremendous suspicion and prejudice. As foreigners moved about the Chinese community they were highly conspicuous by their Western appearance and manners, and the presence of a foreigner outside the treaty ports was enough to incite a riot. Missionaries were not exempt from suspicion as well, being identified with colonial greed, gunboat diplomacy, and opium exploitation of Western governments by the Chinese.

Within a year of arriving in China, Taylor began to seriously consider the possibility of adopting Chinese garb in an attempt to remove cultural barriers and enable him to move more freely among Chinese. Actually, the idea was not original with Taylor, as his predecessor, Charles Gutzlaff, had written articles in The Gleaner advocating:

> The foreign missionary should identify himself with the
> people and their interests; mix familiarly with them, if
> practicable, adopt their dress, and enter into the interior,

not to take the place of a haughty superior, but as far as possible become a Chinese that he may win the Chinese.[1]

Several other China missionaries had also advocated the adopting of Chinese dress, such as LMS missionary, Joseph Edkins, a friend of Taylor's, and the veteran CMS missionary, Walter H. Medhurst. Medhurst himself advised Hudson Taylor to use Chinese dress for traveling in the country. In fact, Medhurst adopted it once on an exploratory trip, but only as a temporary disguise, and had published anonymously an account of the adventure, including detailed instructions on how to disguise oneself as a Chinese.[2]

But to Hudson Taylor much more than personal safety, convenience, or temporary disguise was at stake. He sought greater freedom for his work and wanted to remove any possible barriers to the communication of the gospel. Thus in August 1855 Taylor took the dramatic step and put on Chinese clothes, complete with the conventional queue.

Taylor's revolutionary act created an immediate stir in the foreign settlement in Shanghai. Soon he became the object of ridicule, scorn, and anger. The Western community saw this as gross exhibitionism and a disgrace to the foreign residents as a whole. As George Woodcock put it in the British in the Far East:

> A belief in the equality of all men before God, too literally acted upon, can produce patterns of behavior which no imperial society can accept with equanimity. To the Taipans and all the other people who believed that the white man's dignity rested in strict adherence to British dress and British habits, his [Hudson Taylor's] action was deeply shocking. He had gone native. He had lost face. He had broken the magic ring of white solidarity. The word traitor was not too harsh to describe him.[3]

---

[1]Broomhall, Over The Treaty Wall, Book II, p. 26.

[2]Ibid., p. 279. [3]Ibid., p. 293.

However, Taylor soon began to see the hoped for changes in response to him by the Chinese. He experienced a new freedom in movement and found audiences much more open to listening courteously. Shortly afterwards William Burns followed Hudson Taylor's example and adopted Chinese dress as well during their time of ministry together. In fact, Burns found that Chinese dress had so many advantages that he never again resumed wearing European clothing.

The Gospel Messenger

As a young missionary Hudson Taylor soon discerned that a major barrier to Chinese becoming Christians was that they saw Christianity as a foreign religion. The "strange" appearance of the foreign missionary did nothing to lessen that perception. Thus behind Taylor's adoption of Chinese dress was a growing conviction that the gospel messenger must do all in his power to remove unnecessary cultural hindrances in his ministry and foreign cultural accretions in his message. From a careful study of Scripture Taylor came to see that the missionary to be effective must follow the footsteps of the Lord and the apostle Paul in "becoming all things to all men" for the sake of the gospel.

For Hudson Taylor, however, outward changes in dress were not enough. Rather, as he put it, "There must be heart contact with the Chinese and personal contact too if our lives are to be invested to the utmost profit."[4] Taylor went on to say:

> I do like to look at every practical question in connection with Christ. The Incarnation shows that, provided we keep from sin, we cannot go too far in meeting this people and getting to know them, getting to be one with them, getting into sympathy with them.[5]

---

[4]Taylor, Growth of a Work of God, p. 45.   [5]Ibid., p. 405.

Hudson Taylor saw the missionary primarily as a servant. It seemed ludicrous to Taylor to suggest that it was beneath the dignity of a Christian missionary to identify with the people in outward appearance if that was truly a barrier to communication. The aim of communication, as he saw it, was to build rapport and respect which could only be accomplished through the crucifixion of one's own national pride and the taking on of a servant spirit. He summarized this conviction in a letter written for missionary candidates in 1868 when the CIM was only three years old:

> I have never heard of anyone, who after having bona fide attempted to become Chiense to the Chinese, that he might gain the Chinese, either regretted the step he had taken or desired to abandon the course. Merely to put on their dress, and yet act regardless of their thoughts and feelings, is to make a burlesque of the whole matter. Let us appeal to the Word of God: "Consider the Apostle and High Priest of our profession, Christ Jesus, who was faithful to Him who appointed Him, and left us an example that we should follow His steps."[6]

At heart was the question of identity. For many Westerners, including the missionary community of the time, the thought of adopting Chinese dress was demeaning and repulsive. There was also a genuine fear that the "respect" or deference Chinese would give to a Westerner would be eroded if Western clothing were abandoned and Chinese manners assumed. This was especially felt in respect to the idea of Western women changing into Chinese dress.

In Hudson Taylor's keen desire to see cultural barriers removed for the gospel, he also recognized that ultimately China could only be won to Christ by Chinese, not by foreigners. A great multiplication of Chinese evangelists was needed as well as Western missionaries. Missionaries did have an important role in taking the gospel into the

---

[6]Houghton, The Fire Burns On, p. 115.

unreached provinces and establishing beachheads, but Taylor saw that ultimately China would be evangelized only by the Chinese. As a result, with each appeal for new missionaries there was also corresponding prayer for a greater number of Chinese evangelists to be raised up. Taylor concluded in 1873:

> . . .The work is steadily growing, especially in that most important department, native help. The helpers themselves need much help, much care and instruction; but they are becoming more efficient as well as more numerous, and the future hope for China lies, doubtless, in them. I look on foreign missionaries as the scaffolding round a rising building, the sooner it can be dispensed with the better--or rather, the sooner it can be transferred to other places to serve the same temporary purpose.[7]

A Church for the Chinese

Closely linked to the gospel messenger was also the whole issue of an indigenous church and its role in facilitating the spread of the gospel in China. As mentioned above, Taylor saw the natural limitations of the foreign missionary and realized that the ultimate success of China's evangelization was dependent upon a virile Chinese church rooted deeply in Chinese soil. With a somewhat farsighted view, Taylor saw that Western missions, even though well-meaning, could hinder the spread of the gospel by imposing foreign forms on Chinese Christianity. To address this problem he wrote in 1865:

> I am not alone in the opinion that the foreign dress and carriage of missionaries (to a certain extent affected by some of their pupils and converts), the foreign appearance of chapels, and indeed the foreign air imported to everything connected with their work, has seriously hindered the rapid dissemination of the Truth among the Chinese. And why should such a foreign aspect be given to Christianity? The Word of God does not require it; nor, I conceive, could sound reason justify it. It is not the denationalization but the Christianization of this people that we seek. We wish to see Chinese Christians raised up--men and women--truly Christian, but withal truly Chinese in every sense of

---

[7]Taylor, *Growth of a Work of God*, p. 232.

the word. We wish to see churches of such believers presided over
by pastors and officers of their own countrymen, worshiping God
in the land of their fathers, in their own tongue, and in the
edifices of a thoroughly native style of architecture. . . . If
we really wish to see the Chinese such as we have described, let
us as far as possible set before them a true example. Let us in
everything not sinful become Chinese, that we may by all means
"save some."[8]

Obviously, Hudson Taylor in the 1860s was one of several who
stressed the need of indigenization and contextualization. Close contacts
and a deep friendship with John L. Nevius, the American Presbyterian
missionary, famous for his contribution to the Korean church, perhaps
influenced Taylor in his thinking. Earlier, Charles Gutzlaff had set a
pattern and wrote numerous articles outlining indigenization. Others like
Henry Venn, Honorary Secretary of the Church Missionary Society, published
papers advocating similar principles and saw the goal of mission as:

> . . . The settlement of a Native Church under Native Pastors
> upon a self-supporting system, in such a way that the missionary
> is freed to resign all pastoral work into their hands, and gradually
> relax his superintendence over the pastors themselves, till it
> insensibly ceases. . . Then the missionary and all missionary
> agencies should be transferred to the "regions beyond."[9]

Even with a broad vision of an indigenized Chinese church, Taylor and
the early China Inland Mission were still a product of their day and were
influenced to a certain extent by the patterns of most missions. The CIM,
for example, continued providing support for national workers up until major
policy revisions in the 1920s.

However, in seeking to plant a Chinese church in Chinese soil, the
CIM was a pacesetter and innovator. As an American Baptist missionary in
China wrote in the magazine of the American Baptist Union in 1870: "I notice
that the English Baptist Society is beginning to be influenced considerably

---

[8]Taylor, God's Man in China, p. 187.

[9]Broomhall, Barbarians at the Gates, Book I, p. 329.

by the example of the China Inland Mission. Could not all the old

societies learn some lessons from it?"[10]

Requirements for CIM Personnel

From the commencement of the CIM in 1865 it was understood that all

its personnel would follow Taylor's pattern in adopting Chinese dress and

living as closely as possible in conformity to Chinese customs. This rule

applied both to the men and women of the Mission. The first party to arrive

in China on the Lammermuir changed immediately into Chinese dress and

subsequent workers followed suit. This radical step was especially

demanding for the women, as Hudson Taylor's wife Maria recounted:

> Things which are tolerated in us as foreigners, such as
> wearing foreign dress, could not be allowed for a moment in
> Chinese ladies. The nearer we come to the Chinese in outward
> appearance, the more severely will any breach of propriety
> according to their standards be criticized.[11]

The advantages of using Chinese dress in the interior of China

had already been proven by Hudson Taylor. Thus he demanded a similar spirit

of willingness to identify with the Chinese for the sake of the gospel on

the part of all CIM workers. In the third edition of China's Spiritual

Need and Claims published in 1868, Taylor included an appendix of ten pages

mainly taken from a paper prepared for candidates setting forth the reasons

for this practice. Stress was given not only to clothing, but also to

details such as housing arrangements as well. Taylor wrote in a spirit way

ahead of his time:

> Let us live in their houses, making no unnecessary alter-
> ations in external form, and only so far modifying their

---

[10]Houghton, The Fire Burns On, p. 121.

[11]Taylor, God's Man in China, p. 187.

internal arrangements as attention to health and efficiency for work absolutely require.[12]

The lifestyle of early CIM missionaries was severely criticized by the foreign community in China, who saw them frequently as irresponsible fanatics. Even within CIM there were those who rebelled and refused to make the required changes in dress. However, the great majority did, and it is instructive to read comments from their early correspondence from China and to see some of the struggles and effects of the transformation. George Duncan wrote from Shanghai in 1866:

> I believe with you that the only way of reaching the Chinese is to become Christian Chinese and live like them as far as it is right. It is getting at the hearts of people we want, and in order to do that, we must show them that we are come to seek their good, and not to oppose their customs.[13]

And from a single woman worker, Miss Bowyer, written in 1866:

> We have all adopted Chinese dress, and though I do not admire it, yet it is comfortable. . . . We have left off using plates, knives and forks for the present, and adopted Chinese basins and chopsticks. I thought I should never eat with them at first, but soon became quite expert in them. . . . I do increasingly feel that the more heartily we can throw ourselves into the habits and customs of those around us, the more we shall experience the Divine blessing on our souls.[14]

To Hudson Taylor and the Mission he founded, no effort should be spared in removing unnecessary barriers to the communication of the Gospel in China. He recognized that this was not without sacrifice and hardship. Taylor summarized his heartfelt convictions on identification when he wrote to potential new missionaries:

---

[12]Broomhall, The Jubilee Story, p. 32.

[13]Occasional Papers of the China Inland Mission, 4 vols. (London: China Inland Mission, 1865-1868), 1:21.

[14]Ibid., p. 21.

The Christian missionary has no heaven to leave, no divinity
to lay aside; but as a rule he leaves a home. He has no
nationality which he may claim, and through which he may obtain
many immunities for himself and his followers; or he may see it
wiser to suffer than to do so. He may claim the status of a
foreigner, or he may assimilate himself in dress, appearance,
home, language to those around him. Nothing is easier than to find
objections to this course; but it was the course that Jesus did
take, and we are persuaded would still take through us. The Master
says: 'I have given you an example; that ye should do as I have
done to you.'

---

[15]Houghton, The Fire Burns On, p. 123.

CHAPTER V

INTERDENOMINATIONAL-INTERNATIONAL MEMBERSHIP

Among the several distinctives of the China Inland Mission, the interdenominational character of the Mission stands out in sharp contrast to the church-mission scene of Taylor's day. The CIM was designed to be a special agency made up of members from all the leading evangelical denominations to meet a special need. Hudson Taylor never envisaged a nondenominational or antidenominational organization, but rather one that would be, in effect, transdenominational in order to mobilize the most missionaries and facilitate the speediest evangelization of China. From this perspective the CIM became an organizational pattern for many more interdenominational faith missions to follow.

Factors in Formation

According to J. H. Kane, as the modern missionary movement got underway, several different kinds of missions emerged. The earliest societies were interdenominational, such as the London Mission Society and the American Board of Commissioners for Foreign Missions. These boards, however, still had strong denominational characteristics and were essentially Congregational. Later, various church denominations began to participate in missions and developed their own boards. In the mid-nineteenth century a third kind of board came onto the scene and became known as the faith mission. The birthplace of the faith mission movement was Great Britain, and the CIM was one of the earliest missions founded.[1]

There were a number of factors which influenced and helped to shape the interdenominational character of the CIM. The first of these related to Hudson Taylor's own personal church background and connections. Although Taylor had a Methodist upbringing, yet his contacts with other church groups were wide and varied, particularly after returning to England on his first furlough in 1860.

A. J. Broomhall remarks concerning Taylor's church contacts:

> The nonsectarian, transdenominational principles and practice of the China Inland Mission, which he founded, owed much to Hudson Taylor's early association with the Chinese Evangelisation Society and the (non-Plymouth) Brethren, and especially to his friendship with the ministers and congregations of Brook Street Chapel, Tottenham.[2]

Although Taylor never formally joined the Brethren church, yet their broad outlook and stress on oneness in Christ over party ties, account in part for his ecumenical attitude to Christians of all denominations.

Another factor or influence in the formation of the CIM derived from Taylor's personal experience in China during his first term of service. The missionary community of China in 1853 consisted of only about ninety Protestant missionaries from various boards, and circumstances naturally put them into frequent and close contact. When Hudson Taylor moved to Ningpo in 1857 and commenced work he was immediately part of a close missionary fellowship that crossed all denominational lines. Included among the Ningpo missionaries were those from the Church Missionary Society

---

[1]Kane, A Concise History of the Christian World Mission, p. 94.

[2]Broomhall, If I Had a Thousand Lives, Book III, p. 447.

(Anglican), London Mission Society, American Baptists and American Presbyterians. Not only was there close cooperation, but a strong sense of
interdependence. These positive experiences helped to convince Taylor that
an interdenominational mission was not only practical but desirable.

A third influence in forming the CIM along interdenominational
lines grew out of the reticence of the major denominational groups to
expand or commence their ministries to China. During the years between
1861-1865, Taylor sought to stir the church in England to respond to the
staggering needs in China. Particularly in 1864, Hudson Taylor made every
effort along with Frederick Gough, his partner from CMS on the Ningpo New
Testament revision project, to lobby the major mission societies:

> Mr. Taylor and Mr. Gough made repeated efforts to induce
> the larger missionary societies to undertake a forward movement.
> Separately or together they called upon Rev. Henry Venn of the
> CMS, William Arthur of the Wesleyan Methodists, Trestrail and
> Underhill of the Baptist Mission, Eckett of the Methodist Free
> Church and representatives of other societies, urging some
> other effort should be made. . . .[3]

Taylor even offered to help in the training of prospective missionaries for any board desiring to send them to China. There was some
response from the United Methodist Free Church and the Baptist Missionary
Society, but, by and large, the interest was minimal. The problem of
lack of resources and personnel, overcommitment in other areas, as well
as the current political instability in China, all made the denominational
groups unwilling or unable to do more. Thus Hudson Taylor felt driven to
form an organization that would transcend the limitations of any one
denominational board.

Another influence at the time of the formation of the CIM came

---

[3]Ibid., p. 364.

from the growing climate of interdenominational cooperation in Great

Britian. Broomhall comments:

> The great evangelical revival that 'swept across denomi-
> national lines had two effects among many--love of 'the
> brethren' in other churches, with a new toleration of their
> differing views, and, going a stage further, soft-pedaling
> of personal beliefs about the interpretative nonessentials in
> favor of unity and cooperation on all that mattered most.[4]

Conference centers such as Mildmay and Barnet helped also to foster

fellowship across denominational barriers and a growing number of

undenominational congregations calling their own ministers were

springing up:

> As in the Bible Societies, the LMS and the CES men and women
> of different persuasions banded together to support and to
> send missionaries to work at home and overseas. Personal friend-
> ships overrode denominational labels and many Christians could
> worship as happily with one type of congregation as another.[5]

Therefore, in this climate Taylor's new interdenominational mission, al-

though unique, was still not totally out of place, and in time drew

supporters from a wide spectrum of churches.

Furthermore, the CIM had precedence in a group like the London

Missionary Society founded in 1795 and designed to be interdenominational.

The Chinese Evangelization Society, which first sent Taylor to China in

1853, was also interdenominational, and from that perspective became

the prototype of the CIM. In an article in the first edition of China's

Millions (1875), the editor drew comparisons between CES and the inter-

denominational character of the CIM, outlining the rationale and uniqueness

of this distinctive. The author mentions that although the London Mis-

sionary Society had adopted the interdenominational principle they never

really carried it out. Illustrations of Christians from all denominations

---

[4]Broomhall, If I Had a Thousand Lives, Book III, p. 389. [5]Ibid., p.389.

joining together in religious and benevolent projects, such as the Bible and Tract Societies, could be demonstrated, but the sending out of missionaries from differing denominational backgrounds to evangelize and plant churches within the same society was new and unique.[6]

As the burden of China's unreached millions grew heavier on Hudson Taylor's heart in 1864-1865, the conviction increased also that a new society was needed to reach them. But it was felt by Taylor and those with whom he associated in the newly formed Foreign Evangelist Society (FES) "designed to foster world missions," that any new mission should be interdenominational. One of Taylor's associates in the loosely structured FES, the Rev. J. M. Denniston, outlined a justification for an unsectarian society in a publication called The Revival. His reasons reflected Taylor's thinking at this time as well and are summarized by Broomhall:

> What justification was there for forming an 'unsectarian,' truly ecumenical missionary society like the one proposed? He gave six reasons: it was the true Christian principle; it would supply an object of support for 'Christians who ought to be supporting missions and are not' because of objections to the denominations; for educational and theological reasons there were many potential missionaries who could not serve under any of the denominational agencies; the principle of self-support by missionaries deserved to be promoted; an organization was needed to find and help the no less needed or efficient missionaries from humbler social levels; and finally, such an association could interfere with no existing society, but on the contrary, help all. There is more than enough room for us all in so great a harvest field.'

Thus as the CIM came into being, a classless transdenominational mission composed of men and women engaged in evangelism, church planting and the training of church leaders took shape. Its task was to press into the interior of China where Christ was unknown, trusting God alone

---

[6]China's Millions, 1875:111.

[7]Broomhall, If I Had A Thousand Lives, Book III, p. 398.

and working in the essential unity of the Body of Christ.

Policy and Practice

From the beginning it was understood by all members that major
evangelical doctrines which united them were to be more important than
the minor issues which had led to ecclesiastical divisions. Each new
member of the CIM was expected to be ". . . catholic in their views and
able to have fellowship with all believers holding these fundamental truths,
even if widely differing in their judgments as to points of church
government."[8]

At the same time, doctrinal integrity was emphasized. All candidates had to satisfy the home council as to their soundness in the faith
on all fundamental truths. The fundamentals covered the divine inspiration
and authority of the Scriptures; the Trinity; the fall of man and his con-
sequent moral depravity and need of regeneration; the atonement; justification
by faith; the resurrection of the body; the eternal life of the saved; and
the eternal punishment of the lost. If conscious that any of their views
differed on any of the above fundamentals at any time, members were expected
candidly to inform the Mission and be prepared to withdraw or resign.[9]

Although the constitution of the CIM was interdenominational rather
than undenominational, yet from the Mission's inception Hudson Taylor recognized that differences could not be ignored. As early as 1866 Taylor sought
to deal with this practical problem of maintaining unity, yet preserving
individual freedom of doctrinal conscience. Taylor wrote:

> Those already associated with me represent all the leading
> denominations of our native land--Episcopal, Presbyterian,

[8]CIM, Instructions for Probationers and Members, p. 3.

[9]Ibid., p. 3

Congregational, Methodist, Baptist and Paedobaptist. Besides
these, two are or have been connected with the 'Brethren'
so-called. It is intended that those whose views of discipline
correspond shall work together, and thus to teach his own views
on these minor points to his own converts; the one great object
we have in view being to bring the heathen from darkness to light,
from the power of Satan to God. We all hold alike the great
fundamentals of our faith, and in the presence of heathenism can
leave the discussion of discipline while together, and act as
before God when in separate stations.[10]

This policy was incorporated into the Principles and Practice

of the CIM which was formulated in 1875. The practical outcome of the

policy meant that each missionary in charge of a station was at liberty

to adopt that form of church government which he believed to be most

Scriptural. But once the pattern was set, a succeeding missionary was not

free to make major changes. The P & P went on to say, "The raising up of

self-supporting and self-extending churches must be kept in view. Converts

must be stimulated and encouraged in the study of the Word of God. . . ."[11]

Once the church was under national leadership it was then free to adopt

its own form of church government.

Division Into Fields

In time, however, due to rapid growth of the Mission, consider-

ation was given to the deployment of workers with denominational preferences

into separate fields of work. In this way also the CIM sought to be a

servant and helper of various home denominations by providing them an

outlet for organized ministry in China, which might not otherwise have

been possible. R. Pierce Beaver, in dealing with the history of comity

in Protestant missions, remarked concerning this unique pattern:

_____

[10]Taylor, Growth of a Work of God, p. 416

[11]CIM, Instructions for Probationers and Members, p. 7.

Another unusual development in China was the denominational diversity and adjustment worked out by the China Inland Mission in its earliest period. This pioneer and model of all the later faith missions under the inspiration and leadership of J. Hudson Taylor set out to carry the gospel to all the unreached of the interior then untouched by the denominational missions. Nondenominational in organization, Taylor and his followers thought of the China Inland Mission as truly interdenominational, providing an instrument in which any of the existing church orders might be established in China so long as their representatives would work within the fellowship of the organization, be subject to its administration and accept its methods.[12]

The result of this policy was the development of CIM work in a number of separate denominational fields. Thus Anglicans were assigned to the Mission district of Szechuan, and similar spheres were delegated for Baptist, Congregational, Free Church, Lutheran, Methodist and Presbyterians. It was understood, however, that

. . . so long as certain lines of doctrine and of missionary methods are adhered to, as laid down in the Constitution of the Mission, the Executive of the Mission does not exercise official ecclesiastical jurisdiction over the various churches. In each district the Mission has its own arrangements for the maintenance of the missionaries and their work, and of Mission property. This, however, is distinct from the ecclesiastical government of the church.[13]

In addition to the necessity of grouping workers with denominational preferences together, there were other problems arising from associate members of the CIM coming from continental European societies speaking different languages, having independent financial arrangements and responsible to separate home organizations. Most of these associates represented Lutheran and Free Church backgrounds, and division of the work into separate fields helped to resolve this problem. A field

_____

[12]R. Perce Beaver, Ecumenical Beginnings in Protestant World Missions: A History of Comity (New York: Thomas Nelson & Sons, 1962), p. 113.

[13]M. T. Stauffer, ed., The Christian Occupation of China (Shanghai: China Continuation Committee, 1922), p. 332.

survey in 1918 showed that the denominational distribution of all CIM

church communicants divided in the following way: Anglicans, 3,000;

Congregational and Presbyterian, between 3,000-4,000 each; Methodist,

between 5,000-6,000; Lutheran, 8,000; and Baptist with the highest numbers,

coming to almost 25,000.[14]

Over the years CIM's interdenominational character enabled it to

cooperate with a wide variety of societies and denominations. Its record

of support for inter-mission activities and cooperation in comity is

documented by mission historian R. Pierce Beaver.[15] And yet it is

interesting to note in passing that as CIM planted churches, in spite of

those allocated to various fields, these churches in effect became a de-

nomination and saw themselves as CIM churches.

In an address given by Hudson Taylor in 1889, he looked back with

particular pleasure at the growth of the CIM as an interdenominational

mission. Taylor stated:

> There is one feature of the work of the China Inland
> Mission that affords me great delight, and that is we are
> a little evangelical alliance. We have working in the
> Mission, in the fullest harmony and brotherly love, brothers
> and sisters of all the leading Christian denominations. . . and
> through all the years that we have worked, we have never had
> any friction on any denominational question. This is cause for
> great thankfulness.[16]

International Expansion

Hudson Taylor never intended the CIM to expand beyond Great

Britain as a home country. And yet from 1888 onwards, due to changing

circumstances and pressures from without, the CIM opened its doors wider

---

[14]Ibid., p. 333.

[15]Beaver, Ecumenical Beginnings in Protestant Missions, p. 114.

[16]Houghton, The Fire Burns On, p. 127.

and became international. North America became a CIM sending country

in 1888, with Australia and New Zealand joining in 1890. Members from

continental Europe and Scandinavia also were added, so that the CIM

by 1934 reached its peak (including associates) of 1,368 members on the

active list. In time as the CIM became Overseas Missionary Fellowship

it would internationlaize even further to include members from eighteen

sending countries and a membership of almost 1,000--including twenty-

five different nationalities.

CHAPTER VI

RECRUITMENT OF LAYMEN

When Hudson Taylor first left for China in 1853 he was only
twenty years old and neither ordained nor fully qualified yet as a medical
doctor. His early days in Shanghai were difficult from many perspectives,
but Taylor's trials with the foreign community were exacerbated because of
his ordination status. To arrive in China without proper credentials and
organizational backing was bad enough, but to be there as an unordained
missionary seemed presumptuous at best.

The question of status weighed heavily on Hudson Taylor at times
and forced him frequently to question the value of ordination in missionary
work. Out of frustration he wrote his mother in 1859 asking about obtaining
evidence for his earlier appointment as a local preacher in the Methodist
church:

> [The local preacher's certificate] would be very useful to me
> here, and might help to neutralize the harm done to me by. . .
> some. . . who did wish to represent me as one totally worthless,
> called by no one, connected with no one, and recognized by no
> one as a minister of the Gospel. Now something of this sort
> would show that my call [from God] to preach the Gospel has
> been recognized by the church. The parties who then tried to
> injure me are now friendly enough, but the effect of some
> things they have said and done is by no means removed. . . . The
> title Reverend I do not wish for--but the title Minister of the
> Gospel I do claim, for this is the work God has called me to,
> and is graciously helping and blessing me in.[1]

---

[1]Broomhall, _If I Had a Thousand Lives_, Book III, p. 173.

Through these negative experiences, as well as many positive ones where Taylor proved to himself and others the value and contribution of laymen in mission, Hudson Taylor initiated a bold experiment in forming a mission agency with its membership drawn largely from lay circles. The experiment was not limited to the use of laymen, however, as Taylor took an even more radical step for the nineteenth century by utilizing women, both single and married, in itinerant evangelistic work. Although both steps were highly criticized initially, this dramatic change in recruitment patterns blazed a new trail, which in time many other missions were to follow.

A Rationale for Nonclergy

On Brighton Beach in June 1865 Hudson Taylor prayed for twenty-four "willing, skillful" workers. To him these two qualities overrode all other considerations, including ordination status or educational achievements. He recognized that at times the willing are not always skillful and the skillful are not always willing. But in the right combination of these two qualifications Taylor saw the proper formula for recruiting workers. Speaking in a conference in England he said:

> The man who would attempt to build without an architect would not be very wise. But it would be quite as great a mistake to say because architects are needed 'we will have none but architects.' And so in missionary effort. . . . A bricklayer will build better than an architect, and an architect will superintend and make plans better than a bricklayer. It is in the combination of 'willing, skillful workers,' suited to each department of service, that the work of God will go on as it ought to do. Now we in the China Inland Mission have asked God for workers of various classes, and He has given them; He has given us men of the highest ability. . . . But we have others who have graduated in different schools. . . .
> I say different advantages, for I hold it to be sheer infidelity to doubt that God gives to every one of His children without exception those circumstances which are to him the

highest educational advantages that he can improve and which
will fit him for his work.[2]

From his own early experience in China, and faced with the paucity
of workers in that land, Taylor felt it was both right and necessary to
recruit workers who were not ordained. Naturally he never excluded clergy
from membership, but he was convinced that laymen also had an important
contribution.

To begin with, as Hudson Taylor reflected back in mission history,
he saw where both clergy and nonclergy had been used of God. Examples
like Carey, Morrison and Robert Moffat readily came to mind of laymen
doing effective pioneer work. Taylor felt that in such a large field as
China all types of men and women were needed regardless of their educational backgrounds. William Burns, Taylor's partner in ministry for a
period, had also advocated the same concept back in 1851.

The denominational societies did send out unordained men for
printing or other specialized jobs, along with putting men with limited
education through training courses before ordaining them. But still
the societies' principal recruitment efforts focused on the universities
and the clergy for reinforcements.[3] But as Taylor saw the bare trickle
of "qualified men" going to China, he sensed that there was a much larger
reservoir of manpower which must be tapped for service overseas. Appeals
for missionary societies to send greater numbers to China had brought
polite and sympathetic responses, but very little in terms of additional
workers. In seeking thus to widen the bottleneck for new recruits,

---

[2]Broomhall, The Man Who Believed God, p. 187.

[3]Broomhall, If I Had a Thousand Lives, Book III, p. 248.

Taylor turned to the less educated and laymen for help.

Struggling to meet the overwhelming needs in Ningpo during his first term of service, Hudson Taylor began to envisage ways to multiply workers on the field. He even came up with a "short-term" program of five years of service. He advocated young men giving five years--using the first six months at sea learning Chinese, four years at work, and the last six months returning home! They would work with a Chinese local preacher, living in Chinese style in the country at minimal cost.[4]

At this time Taylor also wrote home pleading for reinforcements and revealed his growing convictions about the kinds of workers who could function effectively in China:

> The language is of the simplest nature, the talent needed does not exceed the power to read and write, and anyone quali- fied to labor among the poorest and most ignorant rustics of England needs only God's blessing to make him useful, or more so, here. I do not either think, or mean to say, that this is the only class needed here, far from it. But we do need, and much need, many laborers of this class. Persons who from the way they have been accustomed to live, are able to endure labor and hardship.[5]

Several years later, in 1864, when Hudson Taylor consulted with colleagues in England about the formation of the CIM, the qualifications of workers became a frequent point of discussion. Comparisons were made with other groups such as the Moravians who had sent out masons, car- penters and blacksmiths as well as educated or professional people. Other missions such as the Chrischona Mission of Basel, Switzerland, had been sending out laymen along with ordained men. Earlier in 1859, M. Spittler of the Chrischona Mission had visited England and advocated the use of laymen:

---

[4]Broomhall, If I Had a Thousand Lives, Book III, p. 198.

[5]Ibid., p. 196.

I repeatedly asked myself, Where is the [channel] through which simple-hearted laborers, who. . . wish to devote themselves to missionary work in foreign lands, could reach their purpose. . . ? All the colleges existing for that purpose require a preliminary education. . . . To raise a missionary agency of a lower kind seems to be a special design of our Lord at this present time, for the carrying out of which He has prepared His instruments in different countries, independently from each other.[6]

Primarily through the interaction of fellow board members of the Foreign Evangelist Society, Hudson Taylor's convictions regarding the use of laymen were confirmed. Only by sending out unordained but skillful, willing workers to supplement the available clergy could Western churches begin to meet the great needs of China. In the words of one likeminded contemporary of Taylor, borrowing military language and describing missions as a campaign, wrote:

We don't send out a mere handful of officers, but whole regiments of rank and file, . . . should we not send out whole regiments of Christian soldiers, not the driblets of a few officers. . . ? Tens of thousands of Christ-loving men and women should throw themselves upon heathen shores to live or die for Christ; and then the enemies of the Lord would become convinced that the church believed in its Lord, its creed and its mission.[7]

Taylor's prayer for the twenty-four skillful, willing workers was answered. Over the years many others followed, the majority of whom were nonclergy. However, in time Taylor somewhat modified his position and the educational standards for workers gradually rose. The Mission took somewhat of a turn in 1885 when the Cambridge Seven joined the CIM, and as a result attracted others of similar caliber.

---

[6]Broomhall, If I Had a Thousand Lives, Book III, p. 394.

[7]Ibid., p. 392.

It is interesting to note that by 1918, of the 960 members of the CIM only fifty-four were ordained ministers.[8] But even a casual glance at the impressive record of accomplishments of the CIM will convince most that Taylor's basic strategy in enlisting laymen was justified. As Taylor himself stressed:

> And when we have found men who are really called of God, let us see that they give evidence of the call at home. We do not put down in our selection of candidates for China any particular level of education or ability that men must have, but we do look out and see that they are men whom the Holy Spirit has used in soulwinning. A voyage across the Indian or Pacific Ocean will not make a man a soulwinner.[9]

Use of Women in Mission

In recruiting laymen or working men as well as others, Hudson Taylor was departing from the practice of established missions. But in encouraging young unmarried women to go to China, Taylor was demonstrating a conspicuous disregard for precedent. From this perspective the CIM again became a pioneer and pacesetter for others to follow.

A brief review of foreign women in China will show clearly the tremendous obstacles which faced Hudson Taylor in 1865 as he began recruiting women for missionary work. In the days of Robert Morrison, Chinese regulations rigorously excluded even the wives of merchants from residence in Canton. The first single lady to go to the Far East was Miss Newell (later to become Mrs. Charles Gutzlaff) in 1827. The first single lady to enter China proper was Miss Aldersey who learned Chinese from Morrison in Hong Kong in 1842, and then eventually settled in Ningpo

---

[8]Stauffer, ed., The Christian Occupation of China, p. 339.

[9]Johnston, ed., Report of the Missionary Conference, London, 1888, 2:17.

where she worked from 1843–1859. She was joined by Burella and Maria Dyer, the latter becoming the wife of Hudson Taylor. Miss Lydia Fay of the Protestant Episcopal Mission, who went to China in 1850, was apparently the first single lady sent out from America.[10]

Thus at the time when the <u>Lammermuir</u> carrying the first CIM party of missionaries, including six single women workers, sailed for China in 1865, there were only fourteen unmarried lady missionaries in all of China, half of them in Hong Kong. All of these were tied mainly to institutional work. Even the role of the missionary wife had been fairly well circumscribed, with wives rarely leaving their spacious compounds except to visit one another.[11]

And yet from Hudson Taylor's earlier experience in China, he saw both the need and the feasibility of single women working even in the interior. Taylor was convinced that if Chinese girls and women were to have an equal chance to hear the gospel, Christian women would have to go to them. And if women in inland China were to hear, missionary women would have to face the hazards as well. Earlier, others like Robert Morrison, Gutzlaff and Lobsheid had advocated the use of women missionaries, but it was Hudson Taylor who would finally implement this strategy on a wide basis.

When the <u>Lammermuir</u> party reached China in 1866 the new arrivals quietly and quickly changed into Chinese clothing and moved shortly to Hangchow, which was to become their first base in reaching the interior.

---

[10]Broomhall, <u>The Jubilee Story</u>, p. 123.

[11]Phyllis Thompson, <u>Each to Her Post</u> (London: Hodder and Stoughton, 1982), p. 51.

The reaction from the foreign community was basically critical. It was bad enough to bring ladies to China, but to dress them in Chinese clothing and send them unprotected into the interior was seen as totally irresponsible.

But the effectiveness of single women in ministry over the next several years demonstrated their significant contribution. These first ladies and others who followed them settled not only in Hangchow, but in other centers such as Nanking, Yangchow and Anking, even in the face of grave difficulties and riots. In time women were a part of advance parties that opened up work in nine of the unoccupied provinces.[12]

A significant development in women's work came in 1877 when terrible famines struck Shansi, Chihli, Honan and Shensi. In compassionate response, relief funds were given from abroad, and some thirty Protestant missionaries volunteered for famine relief work, four of whom lost their lives. With particular concern for orphaned children Mrs. Hudson Taylor, along with two other single women, under escort traveled to the capital of Shansi and worked for a period of time assisting orphans and refugees. This was the first time that missionary ladies had traveled so far from a treaty port. Although the orphanage was terminated later, yet the presence of foreign women so far from the coast demonstrated that there was no insuperable obstacle in the way of women, married or single, residing in inland China. Leslie Lyall goes on to record some of the exploits of these women pioneers:

> The Mission leaders promptly appointed others to the city
> of Hanchung in Shensi, where the work prospered to such an
> extent that an organized church resulted, with a membership of

---

[12]Broomhall, The Jubilee Story, p. 123.

thirty. Single women who ventured into the surrounding country
everywhere found a warmhearted reception. Others made the
long journey to the remote northwest province of Kansu. . . .
Mrs. George Clarke. . . was the first foreign woman to enter
Yunnan. . . . . Thus in the course of five years women members
of the CIM had settled in six of the nine inland provinces,
the first of any foreign women to do so. They were the forerunners of many more, who, facing loneliness and danger,
would self-sacrificingly serve the women of China.[13]

Although the deployment of single women in the interior was a
bold step, yet an even more radical move came about in opening up a
separate sphere of women's work in the Kwangsin River area, running
two hundred miles in length between west Chekiang and northwest Kiangsi
provinces. This innovation grew out of a shortage of men workers. "We
have no men to spare for the fifteen millions of Kiangsi," wrote Hudson
Taylor.[14] And so the question had to be faced of either neglecting the
area or appointing women to the work. The latter of these alternatives
demanded considerable courage, but was chosen as the right course.
Over the next several years scores of single women worked in this unique
field and saw churches, schools and national leaders developed--along
with 3,500 persons baptized.

In 1890 when Taylor spoke at the Shanghai Missionary Conference
he remarked concerning women's work:

The issue of women's work has greatly delighted and somewhat
astonished me; and it is a very serious question in my mind
whether those provinces and others in China which are utterly
closed to male evangelists may not prove to open to our sisters.
We have seen this in some cases. There is not the same fear that
lady missionaries are political agents of the British Government,
and they have been allowed to go to places and to work where
a male missionary would have found no residence whatever.[15]

---

[13]Lyall, A Passion for the Impossible, p. 50.

[14]Broomhall, The Jubilee Story, p. 181.   [15]Ibid., p. 181.

That the principle was sound was seen in its imitation by other societies, and by 1914 women comprised about half the Protestant missionary force.[16] Gustav Warneck commented on this fact when he said:

> The introduction of women in such large numbers into missionary service, even as itinerant evangelists, is due mainly to the growing influence of the China Inland Mission. . . . This mission generally is of epoch-making significance in the missionary history of China.[17]

The Role of Missionary Wives

Unlike the wives of many foreigners in China, CIM wives were seen as partners in the work and were expected to contribute along with their husbands. Accordingly, wives thus became involved in itinerant evangelism and church planting throughout the whole interior of China.

In a letter addressed to the Home Secretary in England in 1868, with reference to new missionaries and their wives, Taylor summarized his convictions of their role and worth:

> It is important that married missionaries should be double missionaries--not half or a quarter or eighth-part missionaries. Might we not with advantage say to our candidates: "Our work is a peculiar one. We aim at the interior, where the whole of your society will be Chinese. If you wish for luxury and freedom from care. . . do not join us. Unless you intend your wife to be a true missionary, not merely a wife, homemaker and friend, do not join us. She must be able to read and master at least one Gospel in colloquial Chinese before you marry. A person of ordinary ability may accomplish this in six months, but if she needs longer there is the more reason to wait until she has reached this point before you marry. She must be prepared to be happy among the Chinese when duties of your calling require, as they often will, your temporary absence from home. You too must

---

[16]Armerding, CIM, Some Aspects of Its Work, p. 36

[17]Gustav Warneck, Outline of a History of Protestant Missions from the Reformation to the Present Time. Translated by George Robson. 7th ed. (New York: Fleming H. Revell Co., 1901), p. 295.

master the initial difficulties of the language and open up
a station, if none be allotted to you, before you marry.
With diligence and God's blessing you may hope to do this
in a year or so. If these conditions seem too hard, these
sacrifices too great to make for perishing China, do not
join our Mission. These are small things to some of the
crosses you may be permitted to bear for your dear Master!

China is not to be won for Christ by self-seeking,
ease-loving men and women. Those not prepared for labor,
self-denial and many discouragements will be poor helpers
in the work. In short, the men and women we need are those
who will put Jesus, China, souls first and foremost in
everything and at all times: life itself must be secondary--
nay even those more precious than life. Of such men, of
such women, do not fear to send us too many. Their price
is far above rubies.[18]

---

[18]Taylor, Growth of a Work of God, pp. 155-56.

CHAPTER VII

LEADERSHIP STYLE

Someone has said that experience is the best teacher. In
Hudson Taylor's case this truism certainly had many applications, particularly when it came to the administration of the CIM. Perhaps at
this point more than any other Taylor's past negative experiences during
his first three years of service under the Chinese Evangelization Society
helped to shape his thinking regarding the ideal pattern for the administration of a mission society. The structure and style Hudson Taylor
initiated for the CIM, in contrast to the typical foreign board of
the nineteenth century, stands out in bold relief.

Emergence of a Leadership Principle

In order to understand the early pattern of CIM's administration it is necessary to review its evolution. The CIM in many ways
had its roots in the Chinese Evangelization Society, an outgrowth of
the pioneer efforts of Charles Gutzlaff. The CES was itself a product
of earlier efforts in Europe and England by supporters of Gutzlaff's
ideas to evangelize China.

In 1844 Charles Gutzlaff founded the Christian Association for
Propagating the Gospel, later to be known as the Chinese Christian
Union, which was designed for Chinese Christians under Chinese

management. At the same time he appealed to European Christians in general to send missionaries to China. As a direct result of his efforts, several German-speaking societies came into being and sent out missionaries to work under Gutzlaff. The Evangelical Missionary Society of Basel of the Basel Mission was the first to arrive in 1846. Shortly afterwards the Rhenish Missionary Society, known as the Barmen Mission, the Berlin Missionary Society of China and several other Berlin-based groups emerged and sought to send personnel to work with Gutzlaff. These were followed by the Pomeranian Mission Union for the Evangelization of China.[1]

During 1849 and 1850 Gutzlaff returned to Europe and England, traveling widely to promote the cause of China and to urge the formation of Chinese associations which would ultimately recruit and send missionaries, as well as support the efforts of the Chinese Christian Union. Broomhall described the purpose of the associations in the following way:

> The object of the association was to select and send the
> right kind of missionary, "not above twenty-four years of
> age. . . (with) a ready talent for languages. . . . They
> ought to be men of the first order in every respect." They
> were to proceed into the interior and take charge of twenty or
> thirty evangelists, setting an example in "preaching Christ
> crucified, constantly, from village to village, from city to
> city, wherever hearers may be found." When they reached Hong
> Kong Charles Gutzlaff would arrange for their welcome, help them
> to learn Chinese and show them where to start.[2]

In Gutzlaff's scheme the associations would not only send personnel, but would also seek to provide support. In response to Charles Gutzlaff's appeals, the Chinese Association in England was formed and recruitment efforts were commenced. In 1850 the Chinese Association launched a new

---

[1]Broomhall, _Barbarians at the Gates_, Book I, p. 311.

[2]Ibid., p. 331.

magazine called <u>The Gleaner in the Missionary Field</u> to circulate news
not only about China but worldwide. The magazine, along with the
Association, only lasted for the next ten years.

Unfortunately, even though the work of the Chinese Christian
Union was discredited and Gutzlaff died in 1851, the Chinese Association
in England carried on the vision, with George Pearse leading as the Honorary
Chairman. <u>The Gleaner</u> continued as well and attracted the attention of
Hudson Taylor. In time the Chinese Association became the Chinese Evange-
lization Society, with the goal of not only aiding missionary work in
China, but also sending missionaries as well. William Lobsheid was to be
its first agent in Hong Kong and Hudson Taylor became its second.

It is important to note, however, that the Chinese Association
and others like it were in a new mold as volunteer societies. Structures
were loose and many of the policies were experimental. For the most part
the boards which grew up to sustain these new societies were made up of a
mixture of Christian professional people, very few of whom had ever
traveled abroad, let alone served as missionaries in foreign countries.
As a result, there was a general lack of experience in administrating a
foreign-based enterprise, and this was certainly seen in the early phase
of Taylor's ministry in China under the CES.

As Hudson Taylor sailed for China in 1853 with three letters of
introduction in his pocket, he had every confidence in the CES that it
would act responsibly in his behalf. Over the next three years, however,
Taylor discovered the hard way that administration by remote control
creates many difficulties.

The CES had insisted that its agents work within fixed policy
guidelines, including budgets and prior approval for extraordinary

expenditures, etc. Strategy plans also had been laid down by the CES

committee in London, which Hudson Taylor was expected to follow in turn.

Although good intentioned, the committee was made up of busy men, and

even the Society's Secretary, George Pearse, filled an honorary position

and had other responsibilities. The committee's total lack of experience

and unrealistic expectations, coupled with its distance from the China

scene, helped to create an administrative nightmare for Hudson Taylor.

Mails between England and China took from three to four months, so that

responses to his requests for help or direction were long in returning

to Shanghai. In addition, Taylor frequently found to his embarrassment

that the CES committee in England reported or commented inaccurately on de-

velopments in China, thus incurring the criticism of the foreign

community.

Finally in 1857 Hudson Taylor decided to resign from the CES, along

with his colleague, John Jones, and work independently in China. Not only

had poor mission management from the homeside precipitated the divorce,

but major differences in policy and financial principles contributed as

well. The past three years had proven to Taylor the impossibility of ad-

ministrating from Europe the work of missionaries so far from home. In

later years, when Hudson Taylor would found the CIM, nothing could shake

his conviction that the final direction of missionaries and their work

must always be close to where they are located.

Headquarters on the Field

As Hudson Taylor responded in obedience to what he felt was the

will of God in forming the CIM, he was concerned from the beginning

that decision-making regarding the work be made on the field. Taylor was also greatly concerned for the welfare of each member of the CIM and wanted to adopt an administrative pattern that would avoid as much as possible the failures and hardships he experienced under the CES. From a practical standpoint, Taylor also recognized that he was the only one in the newly formed mission with field experience, so it was logical that final direction for the work should come from him. As Taylor frankly put it: "I was to be the leader in China, and my direction implicitly followed. There was no question as to who was to determine points at issue."[3]

Initially, the structure of the CIM was quite simple. Taylor directed the field operations and Mr. William Berger functioned as Home Director in England. However, as the number of members increased, and the home and field responsibilities expanded as well, Taylor realized that adjustments in the administrative pattern would have to be made.

On the homeside, due to William Berger's age and failing health, it became necessary to appoint a Council of Management of the Home Department in 1872. The committee, which in time became known as the London Council, was made up of various men who volunteered their time and skills. Later, in 1879, Benjamin Broomhall, Taylor's brother-in-law, would take on the role of General Secretary on a fulltime basis and thus greatly assist the work on the homeside.

As the Home Council developed in experience, Hudson Taylor frequently referred various matters to them for advice and implementation. The principles and practice of the CIM were written by Taylor, but reviewed by the Council before final adoption. The homeside was

---

[3]Taylor, God's Man in China, p. 176.

responsible for recruitment, representation and public relations, although Taylor himself acted as editor for China's Millions, launched as the Mission's major news and publicity organ in 1875.

From the Council's inception, it was understood that the homeside would not seek to dictate field matters; consequently, Taylor had full freedom to direct affairs in China. However, Hudson Taylor, as General Director of the CIM, found himself having to move between home and field in giving direction to the overall work. For almost twenty years Taylor was the coordinator and director, and naturally this put a strain on his time and physical resources. Provincial superintendents were functioning, but Taylor himself had no deputy to act in his behalf during his absences from the country. As a result, a further administrative change was introduced. Hudson Taylor wrote the membership in August 1883 to explain the proposal:

> It is important to secure that no contingency shall alter the character of the Mission or throw us off those lines which God has so signally owned and blessed from the commencement. But our home arrangement of assisting the Director by a Council may be introduced into the China work; the members of that Council may themselves be Superintendents of districts, in which they may in turn be assisted by district councils of our missionaries. In all this no new principle will be introduced, yet our work will be rendered capable of indefinite expansion while maintaining its original character. Many local matters can thus be locally considered and attended to without delay, and local as well as general developments will be facilitated. I have hitherto had the opportunity of conferring only with those of our number who might be within reach and that at irregular intervals. The plan I now propose will, through the district superintendents, bring me into conference with all our missionaries of experience, and will secure an increasingly effective supervision of the whole work. It will also make apparent what has all along been the case--that all important measures are adopted only after full conference with those best qualified to throw light upon them.[4]

---

[4]Taylor, Growth of a Work of God, p. 375.

The China Council soon became a reality, and in 1886 held its first session. The function of the Council was to advise the newly appointed Deputy Director, J. W. Stevenson, who had been one of the first CIM missionaries, and to give guidance to the overall field operation. This basic pattern of administration, apart from minor changes, became the norm until the CIM left China in 1951.

And yet it was at this point that problems were encountered with the Home Council in England. At stake was the issue of management of the work in China. The London Council began to question the role of the China Council, particularly when Hudson Taylor was absent from the field.

> For the relation of the work in China to the Council at home had not yet passed beyond the experimental stage, in which questions were apt to come up that were difficult of settlement. The whole idea of the Mission in this connection--government on the field rather than from a distance--was so new and contrary to received traditions that it was no wonder it had to win its way gradually, and in face at times of criticism and questioning. To Mr. Taylor, with his thorough grasp of the problems to be dealt with, nothing could be clearer than that the control of affairs in China must be vested in men of expert knowledge, leaders in whom their fellow missionaries would have confidence, able to deal with matters effectively on the spot.[5]

It was easy for those on the homeside to have confidence in Hudson Taylor as China Director, but it took time for that confidence to be transferred to the China Council. At the time Taylor wrote to his deputy, J. W. Stevenson, and commented, ". . . the supreme question is that of final headship, and it is equally clear to me that it can only be vested in China."[6] And again defending this position he wrote to another colleague, "We may make mistakes in China, and no doubt mistakes have been made in the past, but evils far more serious would result from

---

[5]Ibid., 506.   [6]Ibid., p. 507.

abandoning what I am convinced are God-given lines for the CIM."[7]

Hudson Taylor had his way and the China Council made up of district superintendents and others continued as the new administrative pattern. Shanghai became the base for the headquarters of the Mission in 1873 and remained there until the Communist takeover. Even as the Mission began to internationalize, the Shanghai headquarters functioned as the central administrative post to coordinate worldwide activities. Although each home country would have authority to function in its own sphere of recruitment and representation, yet field policies were all developed within China itself where the leadership resided.

Centralized Control

Taylor's thinking in administration was in contrast to the accepted practice of most other missions. The success of the CIM from an organizational standpoint is in large part due to the charisma of its leader and his outstanding gifts. Always warm in personal relationships, Taylor was able to command the loyalty of his fellow workers, and Taylor's keen attention to administrative details went far in maintaining confidence in the system.

The CIM developed a pattern of leadership known as director rule. All councils were seen as advisory, with final authority for decisions resting in the superintendents and finally in the General Director. Unlike many other societies, there was no outside board to whom the General Director was accountable other than in a general sense to the Christian home constituency.

---

[7]Ibid., p. 507.

This pattern of centralized control was not without its critics,
however, both inside and outside the Mission. In the very early stages
of the work there was a revolt against Taylor's leadership by several
of the original _Lammermuir_ party. Other outsiders later on described
the style of Hudson Taylor's leadership as autocratic.[8]

Because the Mission was so closely intertwined with the personality of its founder and leader, it is perhaps understandable that diffusion
of authority and leadership was somewhat slow to come. It would appear
even that Taylor himself was reticent to delegate authority as seen by
the slow development of other officers and leaders. Even the handing
over of the general directorship to Taylor's successor, D. E. Hoste, seems
to have been unnecessarily delayed, even with Taylor incapacitated by
illness in Switzerland far from the scene in China.

And yet as a visionary and leader, Hudson Taylor commanded the
wide respect not only of his own mission, but of the Christian public in
general. The phenomenal growth and successful ministry of the CIM from
its inception to Taylor's death in 1905, through the years of tremendous
upheavals in China, would seem to justify his policy of administration.
As H. T. Armerding summarized it:

> The essential significance of this organization, basic as it
> was to the Mission from this time forward, was in its emphasis
> upon the primary role of the governing group in China. Con-
> trary to the accepted practice of other missions, the groups in
> the homeland were subsidiary, and even though the closest possible
> liaison has been maintained with these groups, the final decision
> on Mission policy in the field rested with the China Council.
> While indeed this plan was a novel one, it was not entirely
> theoretical, since Taylor had earlier, in a negative sense, given
> it an empirical test. The very lack of understanding by the
> Chinese Evangelization Society of problems in China undoubtedly

---

[8]E. M. Bliss, _A Concise History of Missions_ (New York:
Fleming H. Revell Co., 1897), p. 245.

convinced Taylor that men in the homelands, no matter how consci-
entious, could not have the essential information necessary to
formulate policy for the field. The success of the Mission
administratively from 1885 would seem to vindicate his conviction.[9]

<hr />

[9]Armerding, "CIM, Some Aspects of Its Work," p. 111.

PART II

HISTORICAL INFLUENCE ON THE

FAITH MISSIONS MOVEMENT

CHAPTER VIII

MODEL FOR MISSIONARY OUTREACH

In the previous chapters an overview of the major distinctives
of Hudson Taylor and the China Inland Mission was given. The question
now arises as to what impact or influence Taylor had on the subsequent
faith missions movement. Hudson Taylor has been described as the
"Loyola of Protestant Missions,"[1] the father of the faith mission
movement,"[2] and the "founder of a new era in missions."[3] At the same
time, Taylor's influence on world evangelism extended beyond the faith
missions movement and touched many denominational societies as well as
the cause of Christ in many Western churches. Upon the death of
Dr. J. Hudson Taylor in 1905, The Christian Herald, a Christian family
magazine published in North America, eulogized the man in a way which
indicates something of Taylor's wide influence: "One of the greatest,
because one of the most useful, of God's servants in this generation
passed from the earth when J. Hudson Taylor, founder of the China

---

[1]Alfred DeWitt Mason, Outlines of Missionary History
(New York: George H. Dolan Co., 1912), p. 96.

[2]Kane, A Concise History of the Christian World Mission, p. 96.

[3]Winter and Hawthorne, eds., The World Christian Movement, p. 172.

Inland Mission breathed his last on June 3. It is melancholy news for the whole Christian world. . . ."[4]

While stating that Hudson Taylor and the CIM were pacesetters in the faith missions movement, it must be admitted that many other factors were also at work in the second half of the nineteenth century. It was an era of great missionary statesmen and evangelical conferences, so that caution needs to be exercised in affording to any one person undue influence. During the years that Hudson Taylor ministered and traveled, other missionary leaders were also spreading their vision and challenges, and thus in the aggregate giant advances in missionary outreach were seen. Yet Hudson Taylor did have a unique place as a stimulus to world evangelism and in pioneering a new form of mission society which developed into the faith missions movement.

Stimulus to World Evangelism

During the early development of the China Inland Mission, a crucial missionary concept was being placed on trial before the Christian world. Taylor set out to achieve what no one else had done, and that was to evangelize all of China. In doing this, unwittingly Taylor and the CIM would become a model for others to follow. As the missiologist, Bengt Sundkler, put it, "In 1865 Taylor founded what was to become the most extensive of all Protestant missions in China, with a name which was both a claim and a challenge. . . ."[5]

---

[4]"Hudson Taylor," The Christian Herald, July 1905, p. 604.

[5]Bengt Sundkler, The World Mission (Grand Rapids: William B. Eerdmans Publishing Co., 1965), p. 136.

It was the audacity of Taylor's faith and vision for the unreached
of China that was to become a challenge to the Christian world. Hudson
Taylor not only described the task, but he set out to accomplish it as
well, and by doing so stimulated many others to bolder and grander schemes.
The church historian, Bishop Stephen Neill, summarized this catalystic
contribution of Taylor and the CIM:

> The great service rendered by the CIM was that it demon-
> strated the possibility of residence in every corner of
> China. . . . Many missionaries did not agree with Hudson
> Taylor's methods, regarding his work as dangerously super-
> ficial; none, perhaps remained untouched by the challenge of
> the mobility, the simplicity and the devotion of the mis-
> sionaries of the CIM.[6]

As Stephen Neill points out, Taylor had his critics. Many felt
that any attempt to evangelize China as envisaged by the founder of the
CIM would be doomed to failure. Eugene Stock, the prominent historian
of the Church Missionary Society, related indirectly some of the opposition that Hudson Taylor generated in the early stages of the CIM:

> But Ridgeway goes on to condemn Alford's proposed new
> mission on the ground that it would be an imitation of the
> China Inland Mission! Hudson Taylor's scheme of reaching
> the unreached provinces is referred to: 'The conception is
> grand; the execution impracticable, and, if attempted,
> disastrous.'[7]

Others criticized the methods of Taylor as being superficial in not giving
adequate attention to the development of educational work and other
church related institutional programs.[8]

------

[6]Neill, A History of Christian Missions, p. 336.

[7]Eugene Stock, A History of the Church Missionary Society,
3 vols. (London: Gilbert and Rivington, LD, 1899), 2:589.

[8]Sherwood Eddy, Pathfinders of the World Missionary Crusade
(New York: Abingdon Cokesbury Press, 1945), 199.

And yet there came in time a growing respect for the accomplishments of the CIM, which served as a fresh challenge to greater efforts in missionary outreach. John R. Mott, the great leader of the Student Volunteer Movement and a missionary statesman with wide experience, pointed out in 1910 the influence of the CIM: "The China Inland Mission in thrusting forth its hundreds of light bearers into the unbroken darkness of the interior of China, not only has been preaching Christ to those who had never heard of Him, but also has stimulated the entire church to more prayerful and aggressive effort."[9] The German missiologist, Gustav Warneck, highlights the place Taylor came to have in influencing missions when he said: "We must devote a somewhat fuller notice to this mission for this reason, that not merely the strong personality of its founder, but also his Christian missionary principles have since exercised a great influence upon wide circles, and have not inconsiderably altered the carrying on of missions."[10] Sherwood Eddy, writing more from the ecumenical context, recognized as well the role of Taylor and the CIM in stimulating world missions. He wrote in a biographical sketch of Taylor:

> The pioneers of the China Inland Mission have led the way
> as pathfinders in entering all the unoccupied inland provinces
> of China. No body of men and women has excelled them in faith,
> courage, in sacrificial devotion, in loyalty to the truth as
> they understand it. No group has furnished more fervid
> crusaders.[11]

---

[9]John R. Mott, The Evangelization of the World in This Generation (New York: The Student Volunteer Movement for Foreign Missions Press, 1946), p. 100.

[10]Warneck, Outline of a History of Protestant Misisons, p. 104.

[11]Eddy, Pathfinders of the World Missionary Crusade, p. 199.

Pattern for Reaching the Unreached

Few missions have been launched with such a systematic and well-researched goal as the China Inland Mission. To reach China's Spiritual Need and Claims is to marvel at the comprehensive view Taylor had of his mission, but also it is to realize that Taylor was challenging the whole church to complete the task of evangelizing China. Taylor carefully plotted the statistics and went on to demonstrate the means by which the task could be accomplished. As Kenneth S. Latourette put it: "In no other land of so large an area and population was there ever a single society which planned so comprehensively to cover the whole area and came so near to fulfilling its dream."[12]

The evangelistic feats of the CIM were not lost on the other boards operating in China at the time. Denominational boards in the early half of the nineteenth century were in the majority and considered themselves as the major thrust of missionary advance. And yet it was the CIM which set the pattern for reaching the unreached. In 1880, for example, W. S. Ament, an American Presbyterian missionary, complained that "We have lost the long-hoped-for opportunity of being the first mission to occupy Shansi. Seven missionaries, three male and four female, of the China Inland Mission have gone into the interior with the expectation of making Tai-yuen, the capital of the province their permanent home."[13]

Yet many other boards took the example of the CIM as a positive challenge. L. O. Chapin of the American Board of Commissioners for

---

[12]Kenneth S. Latourette, A History of The Expansion of Christianity (New York: MacMillan Co., 1929), 6:326.

[13]Marybeth Rupert, "The Emergence of the Independent Missionary Agency as an American Institution, 1860-1917" (Ph.D. dissertation, Yale University, 1974), p. 159.

Foreign Missions commented:

> God is giving them the honor of being pioneers in this
> glorious mission. . . they need to be supported by other
> societies, and it will be a burning shame to us, among others,
> if we do not plant ourselves alongside of them at some points,
> or what is better, strike out in some new lines of advance.[14]

Even prestigious societies like the CMS were influenced by the example of the CIM. Eugene Stock refers to the CIM frequently in his History of the Church Missionary Society. He spoke of the CIM as the "onward and inward" mission, which many other societies, including the CMS, had followed. Stock mentions: "But let it not be forgotten that the example had already been set by Mr. Hudson Taylor and the China Inland Mission. From them the CMS learned the lesson."[15] And again Stock comments: "The subsequent influence of Mr. Taylor upon the cause of China's evangelization--indeed, upon the world's evangelization and, not least, upon CMS' share in it--has been remarkable. . . ."[16]

As the CIM grew in personnel and expanded its operation it came to be the largest society at work not only in China, but for a period of time in the world as well. Within China by 1899 there were fifty-four boards at work, including twenty-three American, seventeen British, ten European and four receiving support from several countries. The total number of missionaries commissioned by all of these boards was 2,461.[17] The CIM, however, made up a sizeable proportion of all China missionaries, with a total of over 700 at that point. Furthermore, their evangelistic activities were so impressive that the influence of the CIM was felt on other groups. Marybeth Rupert remarks:

---

[14]Ibid., p. 161.

[15]Stock, History of the CMS, 2:318.   [16]Ibid., p. 580.

[17]Rupert, "The Emergence of the Independent Missionary Agency," p. 160.

Even those who rather disapproved of the independent boards
had to make an exception of the China Inland Mission in their
discussion of the undenominational societies' errors. The
C.I.M. in turn cooperated in interdenominational councils and
publishing efforts and did not criticize the denominational
missions.

With the success and growing acceptance of the China
Inland Mission, the independents achieved a certain level
of "respectability," which eased somewhat the antagonisms
growing naturally from the increase in the number of independent missions previously dominated by the denominations.[18]

From the beginning Hudson Taylor sought to reach all of the

unreached provinces in China, and the operations of the Mission evolved

from that basic strategy. In the first three decades of ministry in

China the CIM followed a comprehensive plan which included the stages

of planning, extending and developing work within each unreached

province. Initially it was necessary to explore and itinerate. But in

time centers were established and a network of outreach posts developed,

as reported in the China Mission Hand-Book of 1896:

Each of the three decades has its own distinctive features.
In the first the Mission struck its roots in China and gained
experience by opening and beginning to work stations in
previously unoccupied districts of nearer provinces. The second
decade was the one of widespread itineration and exploration of
the more distant provinces, during which the first stations
were opened in all the unoccupied provinces, excepting one,
Kwang-si. The third decade, still incomplete, has been marked
by development and consolidation; widespread itineration has
been exchanged for methodical visitation of smaller districts
around established centres, in many of which churches have been
organized, and in others the fruit is beginning to appear.[19]

Although much could be said about the influence of Taylor on

world missions in general and evangelistic patterns in particular, it

must be kept in mind that other forces were at work creating a climate

---

[18]Ibid., p. 161.

[19]The China Mission Hand-Book (Shanghai: American Presbyterian
Press, 1896), p. 113.

conducive to success. As Latourette states:

> It was a combination of circumstances which gave rise to
> the exceptional dimensions of the China Inland Mission. This
> was in part the size of the Chinese Empire, the fashion in
> which it became accessible to the Christian message in the
> second half of the nineteenth century and the forepart of the
> twentieth century, the remarkable religious awakening within
> Protestantism, chiefly in Great Britain, the British Cominions,
> and the United States, which are usually given the name
> Evangelical and the ability and faith of Hudson Taylor.[20]

But out of Taylor's great vision for the unreached and passion for the

impossible came a challenge to many others in the Christian world to go

and do likewise. In time scores of other faith missions, many with

"inland" in their names, would draw inspiration from the faith efforts

of Hudson Taylor. As Ralph Winter put it:

> Hudson Taylor had a divine wind behind him. The Holy Spirit
> spared him from many pitfalls, and it was his organization, the
> China Inland Mission--the most cooperative, servant organization
> yet to appear--that eventually served in one way or another over
> 6,000 missionaries, predominantly in the interior of China. It
> took twenty years for other missions to begin to join Taylor in
> his special emphasis--the unreached, inland frontiers.[21]

---

[20]Latourette, _A History of the Expansion of Christianity_,
6:326.

[21]Winter and Hawthorne, eds., _The World Christian Movement_,
p. 172.

CHAPTER IX

FATHER OF THE FAITH MISSIONS MOVEMENT

Most mission historians concur that Hudson Taylor and the China Inland Mission were the forerunners of the faith missions movement and a pattern for many other independent missions. Obviously the volunteer society concept had already been in existence, and groups like the Woman's Union Missionary Society of America, founded in 1860,[1] predate the CIM. The CIM also, as has been shown previously, drew concepts and patterns from other individuals and societies, so that there were few ideas which were totally original with Hudson Taylor. But in the alchemy of events of the nineteenth century the CIM under God's blessing demonstrated a viable structure and pattern which drew widespread attention and became a working model that directly or indirectly influenced the formation of other societies. And in this sense Hudson Taylor became the father of the faith missions movement.

The Age of Mission Explosion

In order to see the place of the CIM in relation to the faith missions movement, it is necessary first to draw a wider picture of the Protestant missions movement. William Carey (1792-1834) is usually

---

[1]Burton L. Goddard, ed., The Encyclopedia of Modern Christian Missions (Camden, NJ: Thomas Nelson & Sons, 1967), p. 693.

credited with being the "Father of Protestant Missions," since historians
date the nodern era of Protestant missions back to the publishing date of
his Enquiry. With the formation of the Baptist Missionary Society, a
new movement was launched. The BMS was followed in rapid succession by
a number of other societies, so that by 1824 there were some twelve foreign
mission agencies.[2] In speaking of this new kind of mission structure,
Ralph Winter comments:

> Organizationally speaking, however, the vehicle that al-
> lowed the Protestant movement to become vital was the
> structural development of the sodality, which harvested the
> vital "voluntarism" latent in Protestantism, and surfaced in
> new mission agencies of all kinds, both at home and overseas.
> Wave after wave of evangelical initiatives transformed the
> entire map of Christianity, especially in the United States, but
> also in England, and to a lesser degree in Scandinavia and on
> the Continent.[3]

Organizations for foreign missions in the United States had been
initiated as early as 1787, but it was not until the incorporation of the
American Board of Commissioners for Foreign Missions in 1812 that a major
thrust for foreign missions was sustained. The ABCFM was followed
rapidly by numerous other mission societies, all of which, however, were
denominational.

The independent faith mission came into being about the middle
of the nineteenth century. The first faith missions were formed in
Great Britain and later in America. The earliest was the Zenana and
Medical Missionary Fellowship (later called the Bible and Medical Missionary
Fellowship) organized in 1852, followed by the British Syrian Mission in
1860 (now the Middle East Christian Outreach), and the China Inland
Mission in 1865. In America the Woman's Union Missionary Society started

---

[2]Winter and Hawthorne, eds., The World Christian Movement, p. 187.

[3]Ibid., p. 187.

started in 1860; and the Christian and Missionary Alliance was established in 1887.[4] Most American faith missions came into being during the last decade of the nineteenth century.

There were many reasons why faith missions proliferated and grew so rapidly. Marybeth Rupert points out, however, that the prime reason was not so much liberalism in the mainline denominational churches, although this was a growing trend, but because the founders felt that the full scope of the missionary mandate was not being pursued, whether because of apostasy, indifference, or merely lack of funds.[5] It was primarily the unevangelized fields and unreached people groups, where few or no efforts were being made that motivated the founding of the missions themselves when denominational boards either refused or were unable to occupy them. As Rupert demonstrates:

> It was a common pattern for those who would eventually organize independent missions to appeal first to the denominational boards, which frequently denied their applications merely because the boards did not have any funds to allocate to a new mission effort. This answer was not a deterrent to those who considered themselves called of God to take the gospel to new fields, however. Convinced of God's blessing upon their proposed ventures, the founders of the independent missions determined to support their efforts on the basis of the "Faith Principle" that God could be relied upon to provide all of one's financial needs. For this reason these agencies were known as "faith missions."[6]

Thus, the China Inland Mission came on the scene at a very propitious time in mission history. Even though it was a British agency, it soon caught the attention of many in Europe, Scandinavia and North America. It is significant that in time the key bastion for faith

---

[4]Kane, _A Concise History of the Christian World Mission_, p. 94.

[5]Rupert, "Emergence of the Independent Missionary Agency," p. 113.

[6]Ibid., p. 114.

missions became North America, and it was there that the CIM had high visibility in the late nineteenth century. Marybeth Rupert in her Ph.D. dissertation on "The Emergence of the Independent Missionary Agency as an American Institution, 1860-1917" comments:

> The China Inland Mission, although properly a British
> society, became the most familiar independent agency to
> the American public at large during the later nineteenth
> century. It was constantly the subject of missionary
> analyses and editorials, and figured in every discussion
> of independent versus national missionary organization.[7]

The most publicized and discussed aspect of the CIM, however, was its financial policy. Articles appearing as early as 1879 in The Missionary Review[8] touched on the unique features of the CIM and helped to raise the Christian public's awareness. Hudson Taylor's personal visits to North America in 1888, 1889, 1892 and 1894, speaking in conferences and churches, added further to the CIM's visibility. As will be shown later, Taylor's connections with the emerging Student Volunteer Movement also helped to foster the Mission's image and lead towards the further development of the faith missions movement.

Continental Agencies

Although Hudson Taylor's influence on the North American mission movement was considerable, he also had a great impact in Scandinavia and Europe. A number of agencies were formed from these countries, which affiliated with the CIM in China and became known as associate missions. This pattern was unique for its day and enabled many churches in Germany, Switzerland, Sweden, Norway and Finland to send missionaries to China

---

[7]Ibid., p. 128.

[8]"China Inland Mission," The Missionary Review (London: March-April, 1879), 2:89.

without having to set up their own separate field structures, although in reality these groups did have a degree of functional autonomy in China. And in time some of these societies became independent faith missions, such as the Liebenzell Mission of Germany.

In 1879, when Hudson Taylor was returning to China from England, he held meetings by request at Amsterdam and Marseilles. This was the beginning of many subsequent trips to the Continent, where in time Taylor would become well-known. Later, in 1889, Taylor responded to several long-standing invitations to visit Sweden, Denmark and Norway, including a private audience with Queen Sophia in Stockholm. Wherever Taylor went in Europe he was met by a warm response and strong interest in the work in China. Shortly after this second visit to the Continent--in conjunction with the remarkable ministry of Fredrik Franson, which helped considerably to spark interest in missions both in Europe and North America--several mission agencies emerged and affiliated with the CIM in China. By 1915 there were eleven associate missions within the CIM circle, with a total of 282 Scandinavian and European missionaries.[9] A brief overview of these associate missions will help to clarify the influence of Hudson Taylor on the continental missions movement.

The Swedish Mission in China

In 1882 Josef Holmgren from Sweden visited the CIM prayer meetings in London and there interviewed Hudson Taylor as well. So much impressed by the spirit of faith and prayer, along with Taylor's challenge, Holmgren returned to Sweden and sought to awaken interest in the evangelization of China. At the same time a fellow countryman, Erik Folke, also had contact

---

[9]Broomhall, The Jubilee Story, p. 357.

with the CIM in London and determined to go to China. He was welcomed by
the CIM in Shanghai in 1887 and attended the Mission language school.
In the meantime Holmgren in Sweden heard of Erik Folke and agreed to form
a committee with the purpose of supporting Folke and sending additional
workers to join him in China.

Hudson Taylor's visit to Sweden in 1889 gave new impetus to
missionary interest and helped the committee to further direction and
efforts. Guided by Taylor's counsel, the Committee organized into the
Swedish Mission in China and adopted the Principles and Practice of the
CIM as the basis of the new mission. In 1909 a committee was formed by
Swedes in California to help support the work. By 1913 the Mission had
twelve central stations, fifty-four missionaries, 937 church members,
twelve schools and one seminary for evangelists.[10]

The Swedish Holiness Union

Growing out of a revival in Torp, Sweden, in 1885 the Swedish
Holiness Union was formed and began to send evangelists to needy places
in Scandinavia. Just at the time the newly-formed Swedish Holiness Union
was preparing to send out a new missionary, Emmanuel Olsson, to work
among Muslims in North Africa, Olsson was challenged by Hudson Taylor's
appeal for 1,000 new workers for China. As a result, the Swedish Holiness
Union reconsidered and decided to take up the work in China instead.
Olsson and a young man named Nathaniel Carlesson sailed in 1890 as the
first two missionaries of this mission.

The Swedish Holiness Union became an associate member of the

---

[10]Ibid., p. 359.

CIM in China and worked in Shansi, where it had a special sphere of its own. In 1900 all ten workers on the field were killed during the Boxer Rebellion. Reinforcements were sent, and by 1913 the mission had thirty-two missionaries, with seven central stations and some 500 church members connected with the centers.[11]

The Swedish Alliance Mission

Until 1913 the Swedish Alliance Mission was known as the Scandinavian China Alliance, but was greatly influenced by the ministry of Fredrik Franson as he responded to Hudson Taylor's plea for reinforcements in China. Between 1892 and 1893 about forty missionaries sailed from Sweden, many of whom later lost their lives in the Boxer crisis. By 1913 sixteen Swedish Alliance missionaries were associated with the CIM, working in four major centers in Shansi.[12]

The Norwegian Mission in China

Towards the close of the nineteenth century Norway experienced a spiritual awakening which led to the founding of a missionary thrust to China. In 1889 Hudson Taylor visited Norway, and as a result many were moved to a deeper concern for missionary outreach. Taylor brought up the idea of starting a mission, and the outcome was the formation of the Norwegian Mission built on CIM principles.[13]

The early missionaries of the Norwegian Mission worked with the CIM in Shansi. By 1905, however, due to health problems the mission

---

[11]Ibid., p. 359.

[12]China Inland Mission, China and the Gospel: An Illustrated Report of the CIM (Shanghai, CIM, 1914), p. 32.

[13]Goddard, Modern Christian Missions, p. 492.

practically ceased, but was reorganized in 1910. By 1913 there were
ten workers in three major centers.[14]

The Norwegian Alliance Mission

Through the instrumentality of Fredrik Franson the Norwegian
Alliance Mission was started in 1899 as a Norwegian branch of the Scandinavian Alliance Mission. Its first workers sailed for China in 1900 and
focused work in the province of Shensi in association with the CIM. Regular
work was maintained in five major centers, although the mission never grew
large in scope and personnel.

The German China Alliance

When Fredrik Franson visited Barmen, Germany, in 1889 a revival
broke out, with hundreds being converted. In the midst of the revival
Hudson Taylor's To Every Creature leaflet was published, and this fresh
challenge ignited a keen desire among Christians for missionary outreach
to China. A small committee was formed and liaised with the CIM in
London. As a result the Alliance's first workers sailed for China in 1890.

Later, in 1893, and again in 1897 Hudson Taylor visited Barmen to
strengthen ties and encourage greater missionary efforts. As an associate
mission of the CIM the Alliance grew rapidly and established work in two
provinces. By 1913 there were thirty-seven missionaries working out of
ten major centers, with fifty-seven outstations and 1,369 members.[15]

---

[14]Broomhall, The Jubilee Story, p. 316.

[15]Ibid., p. 362.

The Liebenzell Mission

The origin of the Liebenzell Mission can be traced back to 1891 when Heinrich Coerper, a German pastor, read the German translation of Hudson Taylor's autobiography, A Retrospect. Greatly touched by the book, Coerper later invited Hudson Taylor to speak at various meetings and conferences in Germany. Finally, in 1899, Coerper organized the Liebenzell Mission as the German branch of the China Inland Mission. The first missionary was sent to China in 1900.

In the early years of service in China the work of Liebenzell was an integral part of the CIM. However, in 1906 it was decided that this German branch should be an associate movement with a special sphere of work. As a result the Liebenzell Mission was formed, with Hunan as the focus of ministry. By 1914 there were sixty missionaries in conjunction with Liebenzell operating out of ten major centers, with some 620 church members.[16]

The Liebenzell Mission did not confine its work to China, and in time sent missionaries to Japan, Taiwan and the South Pacific. Later, through the influence of two Liebenzell missionaries detained in America in 1941, the U.S.A. branch of the mission was opened. The name was changed in 1951 to The Liebenzell Mission of U.S.A.

In addition to the above CIM associate missions, there were other Continental agencies which were influenced by the ministry of Hudson Taylor. For instance, the Alliance Mission-Barmen was founded in 1889 by Carl Polnick in response to the challenge of Taylor when he was in Germany

---

[16]China Inland Mission, China And The Gospel: An Illustrated Report (Shanghai: China Inland Mission, 1914), p. 124.

and Switzerland that year.[17] The Alliance had a close relationship with
the CIM in China and worked under their guidance, although the Alliance
itself was autonomous.

The Swiss Alliance Mission founded in Germany in 1889 also felt
the impact of Taylor's ministry and was related to the CIM in China.
Other groups like the German Women's Missionary Union had missionaries
working with the CIM. The Missionary Union was supported by thousands
of Christian women in Germany who met regularly in prayer circles. The
Friedenshort Deaconess Mission of Germany and the Finnish Free Church
also saw the CIM as an outlet for their missionary activity in China.

One of the oldest continental agencies which came to be linked
with the CIM was the St. Chrischona Pilgrim Mission. It was founded in
1840 by C. F. Spittler, who several years before had helped start the
Basel Missionary Society. In 1895 the St. Chrischona branch of the CIM
was formed when they sent out their first missionary to China. Workers
from this mission became full members of CIM rather than associates.[18]

British and American Societies

In the following section the influence of Taylor on several well-
known faith missions founded in the late 1800s will be detailed. In some
instances the involvement by Taylor and others of the CIM was considerable,
whereas in others the CIM acted more as a source of inspiration in an
indirect way.

---

[17]Goddard, Modern Christian Missions, p. 13.

[18]Broomhall, The Jubilee Story, p. 365.

The Scandinavian Alliance Mission (TEAM)

The Scandinavian Alliance Mission was the outcome of Fredrik Franson's work among the Scandinavian churches of the United States. Born in Sweden in 1852, Franson later moved to North America, where at the age of twenty-three he joined D. L. Moody in evangelistic work. In 1888 Franson visited Europe and while in Germany was greatly moved by Hudson Taylor's leaflet, To Every Creature, which was a call for 1,000 new missionaries for China. Franson convenanted to seek at least a hundred of those missionaries, and after helping to launch the German China Alliance, which also became a CIM affiliate, Franson returned to North America and began to recruit men and women from churches in the midwest.[19]

The result was the formation of the Scandinavian Alliance Mission with headquarters in Chicago. Within three and a half months of Franson's return to America a party of thirty-five new missionaries was ready and sailed in 1891 for China. This group was followed closely by an additional party of fifteen workers, making it the largest missionary party to arrive in China in the early history of CIM missions. They and others who followed worked in association with the CIM in Shensi and Kansu in the northwest. By 1913 there were fifty-six missionaries in China working at thirteen central stations.[20]

Franson's burden went farther than China, however, and in time missionaries were sent by the Alliance to other countries of the world.

---

[19]Goddard, Modern Christian Missions, p. 248.

[20]CIM, China And The Gospel: An Illustrated Report, pp. 19, 25.

In 1949 the name of the mission in America was changed to The Evangelical Alliance Mission or TEAM.

Sudan Interior Mission (SIM, International)

In 1893 the Sudan area of Africa was the world's largest totally unevangelized area without a resident missionary among its 60-90 million people.[21] In an attempt to meet that great need, Rev. Rowland V. Bingham, along with others, formed the Sudan Interior Mission in 1898, although the original name was the Africa Industrial Mission. From that time the SIM has grown to be one of the largest Protestant missions in the world, and under God's blessing has been instrumental in bringing into being a strong national church in West Africa.

It is interesting to note, however, that right from the inception of the SIM, the CIM had an influence upon it. During an organizational meeting in Toronto on May 27, 1898, just prior to the formation of the North American Council, the first minute reads: "It was proposed by Mr. Harris that an organization be formed to carry on an Industrial Mission for Africa, adopting the doctrinal principles and methods of the China Inland Mission and similar interdenominational missions. Agreed."[22]

Over the next several years the ties between the SIM and the CIM grew stronger with frequent interaction. Rowland Bingham, who became the SIM's first General Director, had great admiration for Hudson Taylor, and on several occasions referred to him as a model in explaining SIM's

---

[21]Kerry Lovering, "Sudan Inreior Mission" in Encyclopedia of Modern Christian Missions, ed., Burton L. Goddard (Camden, NJ: Thomas Nelson & Sons, 1967, p. 616.

[22]Africa Industrial Mission (Sudan Interior Mission) "Minutes of the Organizational Meeting," May 27, 1898, Toronto.

policies.[23] In 1905 when Hudson Taylor died, Rowland Bingham mentioned in The Missionary Witness, an evangelical magazine he edited and published: "News has come by cable of the death of Mr. Hudson Taylor, the well-known founder of the China Inland Mission. . . . In the Christian church there will be universal sorrow at this loss. . . ."[24] There was a close relationship between Dr. Henry Frost, the first Home Director in North America for the CIM, and Rowland Bingham, as both served on the founding committee of the Interdenominational Foreign Mission Association from 1917 onwards.[25] Ideas were shared and the CIM occasionally served as a consultant, which was true of other mission boards as well.[26]

Central American Mission
(CAM, International)

The Central American Mission was founded by C. I. Scofield, editor of the widely used Scofield Bible. During the 1880s Dr. Scofield was pastor of the First Congregational Church of Dallas, Texas. For several summers Scofield attended sessions of the Niagara Bible Conference in New York. It was there that he first met Hudson Taylor and the seeds for the founding of the CAM were planted. Of that contact with Taylor,

---

[23]J. H. Hunter, A Flame of Fire: The Life and Work of R. V. Bingham, D. D. (England: Hazell Watson & Viney Limited, Aylesbury and Slough, 1961), pp. 239, 234, 236-237.

[24]Rowland V. Bingham, "Death of Rev. J. Hudson Taylor" The Missionary Witness, June 20, 1905, pp. 129-132.

[25]Edwin L. Frizen Jr., "An Historical Study of the Interdenominational Foreign Mission Association in Relation to Evangelical Unity and Cooperation" (A Major Project, Trinity Evangelical Divinity School, Deerfield, IL 1981), p. 6.

[26]Hunter, A Flame of Fire, p. 255.

Charles Trumbull, Scofield's biographer, wrote:

> At the Niagara Bible Conference Pastor Scofield met, for
> several successive years, Hudson Taylor, the founder and di-
> rector of the China Inland Mission. Through Mr. Taylor he
> began to have an interest in foreign missions. This set him
> to studying the Bible to get God's direct word on that subject.
> He saw that the China Inland Mission was wonderfully apostolic
> in spirit, plan and purpose; and he had the rare privilege of
> many talks with Mr. Taylor.[27]

In 1888 Scofield became aware of some of the great spiritual needs
in Costa Rica and shared his findings with a small group of men in his
church, calling them into a prayer fellowship. Later, other survey
work was done on the needs of other Central American countries, with the
result that in 1890 the Central American Mission was organized. From the
beginning the spirit and purpose of the CAM were characterized as evangelical, evangelistic and undenominational. The influence of Hudson Taylor
is seen in the adoption of the faith basis for financial support. Herbert
Cassels remarks, "The mission was organized on the faith principles
pioneered by Hudson Taylor in China."[28] Over the years CAM has grown in
outreach, with some 225 missionaries now serving throughout Central America
and Spain.

South Africa General Mission
(Africa Evangelical Fellowship)

The founding of the SAGM came through the concern of several
individuals in England and South Africa over a period of years. in 1889
the mission was organized by Andrew Murray, the well-known minister,

---

[27]Charles G. Trumbull, The Life Story of C. I. Scofield
(New York: Oxford University Press, 1920), p. 68.

[28]Goddard, Modern Christian Missions, p. 121.

writer and conference speaker of South Africa; and Spencer Walton, a
lay preacher and hymn writer from England.

In the formative stage, however, Hudson Taylor was to have a
small part in helping the SAGM. While struggling in England with the
call and demands of starting a mission, Spencer Walton conferred with
other Christian leaders for advice and support. Among them was Hudson
Taylor.

Walton's first contact came several years earlier when he invited Hudson Taylor along with others to speak at various conventions
Walton helped to organize in England. An article in The Missionary
Witness of September 1915, recounting the story of the SAGM, mentions
the relationship between Taylor and Walton:

> Some years passed by, years of real blessing, during which
> God graciously permitted him to organize some very helpful con-
> ventions at Cheltenham, Ramsgate and other centres of Christian
> life in England; the late Reginald Radcliffe, the well-known
> evangelist and the late Rev. J. Hudson Taylor (founder of the
> CIM) taking part in nearly all of them. Through their addresses,
> and by constant contact with them, the call to go abroad came a
> second time.[29]

In 1888 Spencer Walton visited South Africa at the invitation of
Dr. Andrew Murray and a Mrs. Osborn to hold special evangelistic cam-
paigns. Returning to England, Walton was much in prayer about the needs
and opportunities for missionary work in South Africa, particularly in
Swaziland. Ezra Shank, in writing of the SAGM at that stage recalls:

> In England he conferred with men like Hudson Taylor, the
> founder of the China Inland Mission; F. B. Meyer; and Reginald
> Radcliffe; he enlisted the sympathy and support of a number of

---

[29]Rowland V. Bingham, "A Story of Beginnings: Dr. Andrew Murray
and the South Africa General Mission," The Missionary Witness,
September, 1915, p. 271.

Christian leaders willing to serve as Council members and
otherwise sponsor the new undertaking.[30]

Thus the SAGM came into being, and in time went on to have a widespread

ministry to southern Africa.

Regions Beyond Missionary Union

As one of the oldest faith missions the Regions Beyond Mis-

sionary Union was founded in Britian in 1878, four years after

Dr. H. Grattan Guinness started the East London Institute for Home and

Foreign Missions. Men and women went out from the Institute to do mis-

sionary work all over the world. In 1900 the work overseas for which

the Institute retained responsibility became known as the Regions

Beyond Missionary Union.[31]

The initial field of RBMU was in central Africa. Under the

name of The Livingstone Inland Mission, these missionaries were the

first to establish work on the Congo River. In time other areas of

ministry were opened in India, Nepal and Indonesia.

The influence of Hudson Taylor on the RBMU came through personal

contact with the founder, H. Grattan Guinness. At the same time,

Guinness was of great help to Hudson Taylor and the fledgling CIM in

the early days of its existence.

In 1866 Guinness invited Taylor to join him in Ireland for

special missionary meetings. Some of the first recruits of the CIM

came out of a theological class in Dublin which Grattan Guinness was

teaching in his own home. Guinness gave great encouragement to Taylor

---

[30]Ezra A. Shank, _Fervent In Spirit: The Life Story of Arthur J._
Bowen (Chicago: Moody Press, 1954), p. 141.

[31]Goddard, _Modern Christian Missions_, p. 561.

and arranged deputation openings for him. Later, in 1874, when the CIM

home department in England was established with a council, H. Grattan

Guinness served as a referee.[32]

Four years later, with the encouragement of Hudson Taylor,

Guinness established the East London Institute, which by 1915 had

trained over 1,500 home and foreign missionaries, a number of whom

joined the CIM, including Guinness's own daughter Geraldine. The

location of the Institute was very close to the original CIM home.

Guinness wrote of the ties between the CIM and the Institute:

> Harley House--for more than thirty years our Missionary
> Training Institute--is but a few steps from Coborn Street,
> where Mr. Taylor received his first volunteers for the China
> Inland Mission. How little, when I first visited the small
> crowded home of the outgoing Lammermuir party, did I imagine
> that close to that spot we were to build a college which
> should train more than a thousand evangelists for the foreign
> field. . . . About a hundred of our students have become
> missionaries in China, some of them being numbered among the
> martyrs of the Boxer outbreak. The acquaintance between
> Dr. Howard Taylor and our beloved daughter, Geraldine, which
> subsequently led to their marriage, arose from Dr. Taylor's
> residence in East London while studying for several years
> at the London Hospital. . . . It would be impossible to
> estimate the results for good in East London and throughout
> the world which have followed the selection of that lowly
> dwelling in the mighty city.[33]

About the time the first graduates of the Institute were ready

to leave, an urgent plea for missionaries came from David Livingstone

then in Africa. Responding to this call, several went forth organized

as the Livingstone Inland Mission with the support of Grattan Guinness

and the Institute.[34] Kenneth Latourette described the influences in

---

[32]Broomhall, The Jubilee Story, p. 81.

[33]Taylor, Growth of a Work of God, p. 57.

[34]J. Herbert Kane, Faith, Mighty Faith (New York: Interdenominational Foreign Mission Association, 1956), p. 111.

the development of this new work.

> The Livingstone Inland Mission was largely the creation of
> H. Grattan Guinness and his wife. The Guinnesses had been
> intimately associated with that Hudson Taylor, who in the 1860s
> had created the China Inland Mission, which had as its objective
> the Chinese untouched by the Christian message. The Livingstone
> Inland Mission wished to perform something of the same function
> for those Africans whom Henry M. Stanley's travels were re-
> vealing to Europeans. It came into being in late 1877 and, like
> the China Inland Mission, was undenominational and did not
> guarantee fixed salaries.[35]

The Guinness family was truly remarkable in their overall con-

tribution to world missions. Their daughter Geraldine became a vital

part of the CIM, and through her writings a significant impact was

made worldwide.

Another daughter of Grattan Guinness, Lucy, married Carl Coomb,

who founded the Sudan United Mission. Many students of the Institute

as well made their mark in the faith missions movement, such as Harry

Strachan, founder of the Latin America Mission. In retrospect,

Rev. Joseph F. Conley, U.S. Director of RBMU International, relates

the links between Hudson Taylor and Guinness which produced results for

world missions in other ways: "Guinness, among others, was used of God

to bring into being both the North Africa Mission and the Gospel Mis-

sionary Union. All of these efforts, directly or indirectly, stemmed

from Hudson Taylor's advice to Guinness to the effect that he dedicate

his life to the training of missionaries."[36] The ripples of Taylor's

ministry moved far and wide.

---

[35]K. S. Latourette, A History of the Expansion of Christianity
The Great Century in America, Australasia and Africa
(New York: Harper & Brothers Publishers, 1941), 5:423.

[36]Joseph F. Conley, personal letter 7 February, 1983.

Worldwide Evangelization Crusade

The Worldwide Evangelization Crusade was founded in 1912 by
Charles T. Studd. In one sense WEC is a second-generation mission, in
that its founder was already a veteran missionary from China and India
when he launched this new enterprise.

C. T. Studd was one of the famous Cambridge Seven who went out
to China under the CIM in 1885. After ten years of ministry in China,
Studd was invalided home to England in 1894. But Studd was determined
to work on in the cause of missions, thus he went on to spend six years
in India pastoring a Union Church, followed by a period in Britain and
America pleading the missionary cause among students. In 1910 Studd
left for tropical Africa in response to the great spiritual needs there.
From this fresh act of commitment grew the Heart of Africa Mission and the
Worldwide Evangelization Crusade.

The influence of Hudson Taylor and the CIM came obviously from
the extensive contact with Studd during the ten years of association in
the CIM. When Studd was to found the WEC, the basis of faith, financial
policy and several principles of operation--the financial basis especially--
reflected the convictions of Hudson Taylor and the CIM:

> The funds for this work will be sought from God only.
> Nobody else shall ever be asked for either a donation or
> subscription. No collection for Etcetera work [the original
> name of WEC] shall be taken up at any meeting held or
> recognized by this Brotherhood. If we seek first the kingdom
> of God and His righteousness, we have the word of Christ that
> God will supply all our needs. If we degenerate into seeking
> anything else, the sooner we cease to exist the better for
> ourselves, for the world and for the cause of Christ.
> The Etcetera evangelist must be a man of God and not a

child of man. He is not a salaried servant of the Etcetera
Committee.[37]

Dohnavur Fellowship

Begun in 1901 by Amy Carmichael, the Dohnavur Fellowship was
incorporated in 1927. Initially, the main object of the mission was to
rescue children dedicated to Hindu temples for immoral purposes and to
train them for Christian service. In time evangelistic, medical and
literacy programs were also developed. Amy Carmichael's biography was
written by Frank Houghton, a former general director of the CIM.
Carmichael's own writings, including Gold Cord, have had wide impact.

The China Inland Mission was influential in the development of
the Dohnavur Fellowship and served as a model both in terms of financial
policy and as a source of inspiration. Amy Carmichael wrote:

> The Dohnavur Fellowship owes much to the C.I.M. I have
> often wished that we were worthy to be one of its small
> relations. But the books which so uplift us, humble us
> too, till we wonder, as we read of what men and women of
> God have gone through in China, whether we are missionaries
> at all. And yet India has her cup of tribulation for all
> who follow, even though faintly and afar, the Star which has
> led the C.I.M. from the beginning.[38]

A Model to Follow

The faith missions movement was born out of a great unmet
need, the need of the world's unreached and neglected peoples. Out of
the many faith missions which would emerge to meet this need, a number
were influenced directly or indirectly by the inspiration and pattern of

---

[37]Norman P. Grubb, C. T. Studd: Athlete and Pioneer, 7th ed.
(Grand Rapids: Zondervan Publishing House, 1946), p. 126.

[38]Amy Carmichael, Foreword to Mrs. Howard Taylor: Her Web of
Time by Joy Guinness (London: CIM, 1939), p. 1.

the CIM. The CIM became a prototype then of the new movement.

It is difficult in some ways to estimate the total impact of Hudson Taylor on the faith missions movement. There are a number of societies where a direct tie can be documented, but in other instances nothing is traceable to Taylor and the CIM. Furthermore, without a great deal of further historical research involving considerable effort it would not be possible to demonstrate any clear cause and effect relationship. However, as was mentioned earlier, there were many influences at work in the early stages of the faith missions, and it would be unwarranted to claim more for Hudson Taylor's impact than can be clearly shown.

Regarding Taylor's influence, R. Pierce Beaver wrote, "This pioneer and model of all the later faith missions under the inspiration and leadership of J. Hudson Taylor set out to carry the Gospel to all the far reaches of the interior. . . ."[39] Again, Harold Lindsell in relating the development of faith missions, described the CIM as ". . . one of the oldest of the faith mission boards, whose example has been followed by many other agencies."[40] Harold R. Cook wrote in An Introduction to the Study of Christian Missions, "The first of these interdenominational missions, and the one that has served as a pattern for many others, is the China Inland Mission."[41] In a later work

---

[39]Beaver, Ecumenical Beginnings in Protestant Missions, p. 113.

[40]Wilber C. Harr, ed., Frontiers of the Christian World Mission Since 1938 (New York: Harper & Brothers Publishers, 1962), p. 194.

[41]Harold R. Cook, An Introduction to the Study of Christian Missions (Chicago: Moody Press, 1954), p. 150.

Cook also stated:

> Before the end of the century there were other interde-
> nominational missions, more or less patterned after the
> China Inland Mission: The Regions Beyond Missionary Union,
> the Cape General Mission (now Africa Evangelical Fellowship),
> the Central American Mission, the Scandinavian (now
> Evangelical) Alliance, the Sudan Interior Mission, the Africa
> Inland Mission and others.[42]

In the next chapter it will be shown how Taylor contributed to

the Student Volunteer Movement, which in turn did so much to feed the

faith missions movement.

---

[42]Harold R. Cook, _Highlights of Christian Missions_ (Chicago:
Moody Press, 1967), p. 66.

CHAPTER X

IMPACT ON THE STUDENT MISSIONS MOVEMENT

In 1886 a remarkable movement was launched in North America which came to have a tremendous impact on world missions. Under God this movement, known as the Student Volunteer Movement for Foreign Missions, helped to propel over 20,000 new missionaries into foreign lands.[1] In addition, thousands more made commitments to support and pray for missions. Thus the SVMFM became a significant factor in the world missionary enterprise and contributed immensely to the progress of the gospel.

Links in a Chain

There were many factors that contributed to the formation of the SVM and its success in mobilizing students for missions over the years. One of the links in the chain, however, which led to the creation of the SVM, was tied to Hudson Taylor and the China Inland Mission. Events which took place in England two years prior to the Mt. Hermon, Massachusetts, conference of 1886 that launched the movement became part of the chain which eventually brought the movement into being.

---

[1]David M. Howard, Student Power in World Missions, 2d ed. (Downers Grove, IL: Intervarsity Press, 1979), p. 97.

The Cambridge Seven

When D. L. Moody responded to the invitation to visit England for evangelistic meetings in 1882, little did anyone realize the impact he would have there on the student world. In November 1882 Moody and Sankey conducted an eight-day mission at Cambridge University with surprising results. As a direct outcome of the meetings a number of students were converted, but in addition a new sense of missionary zeal was imparted as well.

Among the converts and those influenced by Moody's ministry were D. E. Hoste of the Royal Artillery; C. T. Studd, the Cambridge cricket captain; Stanley Smith, stroke of the Cambridge boat; and Montague Beauchamp, heir to a baronetcy and stroke of one of the trial eights. Also challenged at that time were William Cassels, a Cambridge graduate and Anglican curate; and Arthur and Cecil Turner, sons of a prominent member of Parliament.

All of these men were brilliant and talented, with outstanding backgrounds. Over the course of the next year, however, they were drawn by the claims of China's unreached millions, and applied to the China Inland Mission in October 1884. Such an unusual, and even startling event captured both the headlines and the public imagination. Cambridge University itself was greatly stirred, and the group became known as the Cambridge Seven.

Before leaving for China, however, farewell meetings were arranged in several places. The response was overwhelming and created interest throughout the country. Never had a group of young men so prominent in the sporting world and so distinguished socially, sailed at one time to become missionaries. Eugene Stock, historian

of the Church Missionary Society, described the impact in the following

way:

> The influence of such a band of men going to China as
> missionaries was irresistible. No such event had occurred
> before; and no event of the century had done so much to
> arouse the minds of Christian men to the tremendous claims
> of the field, and the nobility of the missionary vocation.
> The gift of such a band to the China Inland Mission--truly
> it was a gift from God--was a just reward to Mr. Hudson
> Taylor and his colleagues for the genuine unselfishness with
> which they had always pleaded the cause of China and the
> world, and not of their own particular organization, and for
> the deep spirituality which has always marked their meetings.
> And that spirituality marked most emphatically the densely-
> crowded meetings in different places at which these seven
> men said farewell.
> . . . . In many ways the Church Missionary Society owes
> a deep debt of gratitude to China Inland Mission and the
> Cambridge Seven. The Lord Himself spoke through them; and
> it was by His grace that the Society had ears to hear.[2]

The issue of the China's Millions which contained the report

of the final farewell meeting at Exeter Hall went into 50,000 copies

because of demand and was widely circulated.[3] As a follow-up, a

special book was published entitled A Missionary Band: A Record and an

Appeal. This book gave further details and testimonies of the Cambridge

Seven and likewise enjoyed wide circulation. Fifteen thousand copies

were rapidly sold, and a copy was even accepted by Her Majesty Queen

Victoria.[4] An enlarged and improved edition under the title of

The Evangelization of the World was published and also had considerable

impact. A copy was sent by Sir George Williams, along with a personal

letter, to every YMCA in the United Kingdom. Later, Dr. Robert Speer

---

[2]Stock, History of the CMS, 2:284.

[3]Lyle, A Passion for the Impossible, p. 55.

[4]Broomhall, The Jubilee Story, p. 166.

of the SVM publicly stated that apart from the Bible no books had so greatly influenced his career as Dr. Baikie's Personal Life of Living-stone and Broomhall's Evangelization of the World.[5]

J. E. K. Studd

News of the Cambridge Seven traveled outside of England as well. In the United States interest was aroused, and in 1885 D. L. Moody invited J. E. K. Studd, C. T. Studd's brother and organizer of Moody's Cambridge mission in England, to visit America and tell of God's unusual work in Great Britain.

Shortly after Studd arrived in Northfield, Massachusetts, at Moody's conference center, he came into contact with Luther Wishard and his new assistant, Charles Ober. Upon hearing of the student movement in Britain Wishard and Ober longed to see something similar happen among American students. With Moody's help they convinced Studd to tour American colleges, telling the story of the Cambridge Seven. Studd spent over three months speaking at twenty different colleges and several intercollegiate conferences as well.[6] Of particular significance was J. E. K. Studd's visit to Cornell University, where he encountered a young student by the name of John R. Mott. Mott in time became the leader in the SVM and had a tremendous influence on world missions.

Out of the Mt. Hermon summer conference at Northfield in 1885 the idea of a special Bible conference for students under Moody's

---

[5]Ibid., p. 166.

[6]Timothy C. Wallstrom, The Creation of a Student Movement to Evangelize the World (Pasadena: William Carey Int'l Univ. Press, 1980), p. 38.

teaching at Mt. Hermon crystallized. The conference was scheduled for
July 1886, and a total of 251 students from eighty-nine colleges of the
U.S. and Canada attended.[7] Although the Bible conference was not
initially slanted towards world missions, yet towards the close of the
meetings Dr. A. T. Pierson, an authority and advocate of missions, was
requested by Robert Wilder and other students to give a missionary address. The conference took a significant turn at that stage and missions
increasingly became the focal point of discussion. As a result of the
Mt. Hermon conference one hundred of the students attending indicated
a willingness to serve as foreign missionaries by signing the
Princeton Pledge, which stated: "It is my purpose, if God permit, to
become a foreign missionary."[8]

The Volunteer Movement

Following the close of the successful Mt. Hermon conference,
careful thought and prayer were given as to how this new mission vision
could be passed on to other students and the infant movement could be
kept alive. John R. Mott records later the way in which the Cambridge
Seven deputations became a model and inspiration for fostering the
student movement in North America:

> At this final meeting there was a unanimous expression
> that the missionary spirit which had manifested itself with
> such power at Mt. Hermon should be communicated, in some
> degree at least, to the thousands of students in the
> colleges and seminaries who had not been privileged to come
> in contact with it at its source. It was the conviction of
> the volunteers that the reasons which had led them to decide
> would influence hundreds of other students, if those reasons
> were once presented to them in a practical, intelligent,

---

[7]Ibid., p. 41.

[8]Howard, Student Power in World Missions, p. 95.

faithful and prayerful manner. Two days before this suggestion had come to a few of the volunteers and leaders of the conference, while on a tramp over the hills near the Vermont border, that a deputation, something like the Cambridge Band, be sent among the colleges. This famous band was composed of seven Cambridge students noted for their scholarship, their prominence in athletics, and above all, their consecration and spirituality. Before going out to China they made a memorable tour among the British Universities, creating a great missionary revival among the students-- felt also more or less by the entire church. When this plan was mentioned to the volunteers it was heartily and prayerfully adopted.[9]

Over the school year of 1886-87, Robert Wilder and John Forman, also of Princeton University, traveled to 162 institutions challenging students towards missions. By the end of the year they had seen 2,106 students sign the Volunteer Declaration, of whom about 500 were women.[10] In time the SVMFM was incorporated into the structures of the YMCA, YWCA and Inter-Seminary Missionary Alliance to give it stability and continuity. National conferences were held every four years and this pattern continued until after World War II.

After the inauguration of the Student Volunteer Movement in North America, Wilder and Forman also traveled to Great Britain to share God's working among students. Their visit directly helped to start the Student Volunteer Missionary Union of the British Isles, which contributed significantly to the missions thrust from Britain. Under the organization's influence several thousands of student volunteers sailed in connection with the various missionary societies. The visit of Wilder and Forman had an influence in quickening missionary interest in Scandinavia, and later other students helped to transplant

---

[9]John R. Mott, Addresses and Papers of John R. Mott, Student Volunteer Movement for Foreign Missions (New York: Association Press, 1946), 1:6.

[10]Howard, Student Power in World Missions, p. 92.

the movement to Australia, New Zealand and other countries.[11]

Hudson Taylor's Visits to North America

In 1886, at the invitation of D. L. Moody, Hudson Taylor came to North America to speak at the Northfield and Niagara conferences as well as at other places. The Student Volunteer Movement was only two years old but gaining momentum and Taylor was willing to encourage it in any way possible. Hudson Taylor wrote later in reflection:

> I was glad to come when my way was providentially opened. I wanted to see Mr. Moody, and had heard of over 2,000 students wishful to consecrate their lives to God's service abroad. The American societies, I thought, are not quite in a position to take up these 2,000, and perhaps if we tell them about God's faithfulness they will find it written in their Bibles not "be sent" but "go". I believe in verbal inspiration, and that God could have said "be sent" if He had wished it, instead of "go". I hoped I might be able to encourage some to "go".[12]

When Taylor arrived in Northfield in August, the student conference was in full swing. Among the students were some fifty student volunteers as well. At this point, however, the Student Volunteer Movement was in danger of stalling or fragmenting, due to lack of leadership and structure. Prayerful concern was expressed also for the many institutions which had not been reached yet.

In this context Taylor came and ministered the Word along with Moody and others. Four hundred men from ninety different colleges filled the building and overflowed in tents. The audience included many pastors, professors and YMCA secretaries. These meetings were greatly

---

[11]Mott, _Addresses and Papers of John R. Mott_, 1:186.

[12]Taylor, _God's Man in China_, p. 295.

blessed, and became a turning point not only for many individuals but also for the fledgling SVMFM. Robert Wilder wrote of the impact of Taylor at that conference:

> With the exception of my own father, Mr. Taylor was the man who was the greatest spiritual help to me. When he came to Northfield and appealed on behalf of China, the hearts of the delegates burned within them, and he not only made the needs of the mission field very real; he showed us the possibilities of the Christian life. The students loved to hear him expound the Word of God. He was a master of his Bible, and his sympathy and naturalness attracted men to him. His addresses were so much appreciated that Mr. Moody had to announce extra meetings to be held by him in the afternoons-- so many of the students were anxious to hear from the veteran missionary. . . . Eternity alone can reveal the results of that life, and the effect of his words upon our Student Movement.

Out of this rich time in the Word and prayer, inspiration came to Charles Ober as to a form of organization which might give the Movement the needed structure and stability. As a result, Ober's plan was implemented, and the Student Volunteer Movement was henceforth tied to teh YMCA, YWCA and the Inter-Seminary Alliance.

From this first visit to North America, another surprise awaited Hudson Taylor. Out of the new mission interest generated at the Niagara Conference and elsewhere, monies and offers of service for China with the CIM poured in. Although Taylor had been urged to open an American branch of the CIM earlier by Henry Frost, now Hudson Taylor was forced to evaluate afresh God's plans with the presence of recruits and funds to send them forth. Thus, within a span of several weeks, a new chapter was opened in the organizational history of the Mission, with the result that the CIM became international with the establishment of a North American branch. In time Henry W. Frost became the

---

[13]Ibid., p. 296.

first North American Home Director and saw hundreds of recruits go out
to China with the CIM.

In 1894 Hudson Taylor returned to America for further ministry
on his way to China for the ninth time. A highlight of this visit was
his appearance at the Second International Convention of the SVMFM
held February 28-March 4, 1894, in Detroit, Michigan. Some 1,082
students attended, representing 294 institutions of Canada and the
United States.[14] Hudson Taylor had major addresses throughout the
conference and his ministry was greatly appreciated. Here he exerted
a strong influence on such men as Robert Wilder, Robert E. Speer,
John R. Mott and hundreds of other students.

Of special significance during the conference was an unscheduled
early morning meeting when Taylor shared informally of his own spiritual
experiences, and in particular the secret of abiding in Christ and the
exchanged life:

> The message was the same that had brought help to many in
> Shanghai two years previously, and as then, heart after heart
> discovered God's provision to meet all depths of failure and
> need. Years of devoted service on many a mission field were
> to bear witness to the spiritual transactions of that hour.[15]

Among the students who were greatly challenged and helped was
Samuel Zwemer, pioneer missionary statesman, writer and apostle to
Islam. At the SVM convention in Kansas City, 1914, Zwemer also testi-
fied to a life-changing experience at Detroit through the ministry of

---

[14]Max Wood Moorhead, ed., The Student Missionary Enterprise:
The Second International Convention of the Student Volunteer Movement,
1894 (Boston: T. O. Metcalf & Co., 1894), pp. 362-364.

[15]Taylor, God's Man in China, p. 328.

Hudson Taylor.[16]

In later years Taylor's example as a man of God and committed missionary was frequently held up to students attending SVM conventions. John R. Mott saw Hudson Taylor and the China Inland Mission as a model worthy to be followed, and in his leadership in the Student Volunteer Movement Mott often challenged students with illustrations taken from Taylor's experiences. Another early leader in the SVM, and a prominent missionary to India, John Forman, summarized well the impact of Taylor on the student movement in America during its development: "One of the greatest blessings of my life came to me through, not from, the Rev. J. Hudson Taylor. . . . He was a channel--open, clean, and so closely connected with the Fountain of Living Waters that all who came in contact with him were refreshed."[17]

The SVM and Faith Missions

In the early stages of the SVM most volunteers went out with existing denominations primarily because, apart from the CIM, there were very few faith boards in existence. However, almost half of the volunteers who went out in the first twenty years of the movement went to China and India, reflecting some of the influence of Hudson Taylor and other CIM spokesmen in the early stages.[18]

---

[16]Fennell P. Turner, ed., Students and the World-Wide Expansion of Christianity: The Seventh International Convention of the Student Volunteer Movement, 1914 (New York: Student Volunteer Movement for Foreign Missions, 1914), p. 634.

[17]Taylor, Growth of a Work of God, p. 444.

[18]Wallstrom, Creation of a Student Movement, p. 65.

During the period from 1900 to 1920, about three-quarters of the male and unmarried female missionaries going out from North America had signed the volunteer pledge.[19]   It is evident, therefore, that the Student Volunteer Movement had a major role in securing commitments from roughly one-half of the total missionaries leaving from America during the first two decades of the twentieth century. Furthermore, many other new missionaries were probably influenced by the Movement in either a secondary or indirect way. And, as was mentioned earlier, the SVM in North America went on to influence and inspire numerous other movements elsewhere. Thus, in the combination of forces, Hudson Taylor had a part in spawning and influencing a major student movement which impacted greatly on world missions, including the faith missions movement.

---

[19]Ibid., p. 83.

CHAPTER XI

CONFERENCES AND PUBLICATIONS

The influence of Hudson Taylor extended far beyond China. As Robert Wilder expressed it in 1906 following Taylor's death: "And Christian friends, when the secrets are revealed, it may be seen that that man of God has accomplished more outside of the China Inland Mission than within the circle of its influence."[1] For Hudson Taylor was more than a missionary or an administrator; he was in fact a missionary statesman and a teacher of the Word. As such Taylor was frequently called upon to participate in conferences, and in this way he influenced many.

Conference Ministry

A man with an ecumenical heart, Taylor was always interested in sharing and cooperating with others of like evangelical mind in causes which would advance the work of Christ. Over the years Hudson Taylor helped to promote and participated in a number of major mission conferences focusing on issues, problems and strategy of missions. Several conferences of strategic importance will be highlighted now.

Shanghai General Conference--1877

In May 1877 Shanghai was the venue of a significant

---

[1]Houghton, The Fire Burns On, p. 31.

inter-mission conference of missionaries. More than 120 gathered together for two weeks to discuss issues of major concern and to
strengthen God's work in China.[2] This was the first conference of its
kind in China, and Hudson Taylor was invited to give a strategy paper.

The atmosphere preceding the conference had been somewhat tense
due to the so-called "term question,"[3] and some missionaries had held
aloof, feeling that the conference might end in controversy and strife.
A further source of tension was over methodology in terms of itinerant
versus local settled work. Hudson Taylor and the China Inland Mission
had already received widespread criticism over the long itinerations
taken by some members, which were seen as wasteful, and perhaps even
counterproductive.

The Shanghai Conference convened with about one-fifth of the
total missionaries working in China present. They represented all of
the major societies, and thus lent unusual importance to this first
General Conference of Protestant Missionaries in China. Among the many
topics discussed were critical subjects such as the role of medical
missions, missions and education, self-support of native churches,
employment of native assistants, ancestral worship, Christianity and
Confucianism, church leadership training and methods of evangelism.
Papers were also read on the social issues of opium and footbinding.
Coming out of this conference was a strong appeal to Western

---

[2]China's Millions, 1877:111.

[3]The debate as to what Chinese term should be adopted as the
nearest and most unambiguous equivalent for the Scriptural idea of God.

churches for the sending of more missionaries.[4]

Even though Hudson Taylor's paper on "Itineration Far and Near as an Evangelizing Agency" was controversial, yet it was received well and, as the Celestial Empire recorded, ". . . secured the deepest interest of the audience."[5] Evidently Taylor's participation in the conference helped to break down barriers of suspicion and criticism of the CIM. Even the Chinese dress of Taylor and his fellow workers ceased to offend, and the "forward movement they represented had passed into the confidence and prayerful sympathy of most if not all present."[6]

Centenary Conference, London--1888

A landmark missions conference was held in London, June 9-19, 1888, known as the Centenary Conference on Foreign Missions. In attendance were some 1,579 missionaries and representatives of 140 mission agencies.[7] The conference was not only significant for the participants, but made such an impact upon the public of Great Britain that missionary giving increased by forty percent between 1888 and 1890.[8]

The primary purpose of the conference was to stimulate and encourage all evangelistic agencies to press ahead in fulfilling the Great Commission. To help facilitate this purpose, the conference

---

[4]Records of the General Conference of the Protestant Missionary in China (Shanghai: American Presbyterian Mission Press, 1877).

[5]Taylor, Growth of a Work of God, p. 299. [6]Ibid., p. 299.

[7]Johnston, ed., Report on the Missionary Conference (New York: Fleming H. Revell, 1888), 1:XIV.

[8]Arthur Johnston, The Battle for World Evangelism (Wheaton: Tyndale House Publishers, Inc., 1978), p. 28.

approved the following guidelines:

> The means proposed for the accomplishment of this great
> object are to take advantage of the experience of the last
> hundred years of Protestant missions, in the light of God's
> Word, by gathering together Christians of all Protestant com-
> munities engaged in missionary labours throughout the world,
> to confer with one another on those many important and delicate
> questions which the progress of civilisation and the large
> expansion of missionary work have brought into prominence, with
> a view to develop the agencies employed for the spread of the
> 'Gospel of the grace of God.' The ends aimed at may be classed
> under three heads.
> 1st. To turn to account the experience of the past for
> the improvement of the methods of missionary enterprise in
> the foreign field.
> 2nd. To utilise required experience for the improvement
> of the methods for the home management of foreign missions.
> 3rd. To seek the more entire CONSECRATION OF THE CHURCH
> OF GOD in all its members to the great work committed to it
> by the Lord.[9]

The scope of the conference was broad in reporting on the state

of missions worldwide, although discussions were focused on eight

principal areas. The topics were: missionary methods, medical missions,

women's missions to women, the place of education in missions, litera-

ture in missions, organization of native churches, the work at home and

mission comity. There were thirty-one delegates from the CIM, and Hudson

Taylor had a significant part in the conference.

Among several topics, Taylor presented a major paper on itineration

in evangelistic work. This paper was essentially the same as the one

presented back at the 1877 Shanghai General Conference. In addition,

Hudson Taylor made presentations on the opium traffic problem,

China as a mission field, qualifications of a missionary, the evils of

proselytizing and polygamy. The high visibility of Taylor throughout

the conference was indicative of his growing stature as a missionary

---

[9]Johnston, _Report of the Missionary Conference_, London, 1888,
1:viii.

spokesman. The CIM was also reaching a high point of public awareness with the sailing of the Cambridge Seven in 1885, and then The Hundred in 1887 just prior to the London Conference. The CIM now numbered almost 300 in membership and was one of the largest societies of the day.

Shanghai General Conference--1890

In May 1890 a Second General Conference of China Missionaries was held in Shanghai. Some 445 missionaries assembled out of the total of 1,295 then resident in China. This represented a proportional increase in participation from the earlier 1877 General Conference. Over thirty-three mission societies sent representatives, with the China Inland Mission represented by a total of eighty-four, the largest delegation of any board present.[10]

Some sixty papers were read, covering nine general subjects. The key topics focused on Chinese versions of the Bible, the missionary, women's work, medical work, the native church, education, literature, ancestral worship and comity in missions. Out of the discussions, agreement was finally reached on a union version of the Chinese Bible. W. A. P. Martin's paper on ancestral worship provoked considerable controversy, and his conclusions were denounced by the conference in the form of a resolution.[11] Hudson Taylor presented several papers during the conference, but his opening message set the tone for the meetings and resulted in a conference appeal which had worldwide impact.

---

[10]Records of the Missionary Conference, Shanghai, 1890, p. xxiii.

[11]Ibid., p. lxiii.

For months prior to the Shanghai Conference, Hudson Taylor had been greatly exercised over the still unevangelized millions of China. Challenged by this unmet need, Taylor wrote a pamphlet entitled To Every Creature, which called for the evangelization of China. This pamphlet went on to have wide circulation and resulted in the stirring up of considerable response and missionary offers from numerous Western countries.

When Taylor preached the opening sermon at the Shanghai conference, he drew principles from the story of Jesus feeding the multitudes, reinforcing his proposed plan to preach the gospel in every district, town and village of China. Hudson Taylor maintained that the current number of 49,000 Protestant converts was far too small, and new outreach was imperative and possible. He proceeded to suggest the adoption of a united appeal from the conference calling for a thousand new missionaries. These new missionaries should be men, coming out with all the different societies for various work in China within the next five years. The conference adopted the suggestion and issued the appeal.

The appeal for The Thousand met with an enthusiastic response from Europe especially where the churches were in the midst of spiritual revival. Over the next five years all societies experienced an influx of new workers, but the CIM in particular received the largest intake. In the five months between October 1890 and March 1891 alone, no fewer than 126 new workers arrived in China to work with the CIM. Many of these came through the influence of Fredrik Franson. Five years after the appeal it was estimated that 1,153 new workers had arrived in China under all missions. The prayer for 1,000 men, however, was not seen totally, as 672 of the number were women.[12]

Ecumenical Missionary Conference
New York, 1900

At the outset of the twentieth century an outstanding missionary

conference was held in April 1900 at Carnegie Hall in New York City.

In addition to the 1,500 delegates from 400 societies, some esti-

mated 200,000 people attended the various sessions of the ten-day

conference.[13]

The conference was designed to cover a number of strategic

subjects, with a view to presenting the differing points of view.

Although surveys of the various mission fields were presented, the major

direction of the conference was structured in the following way:

> The controlling thought in the construction of the pro-
> gramme was not so much to arrange a series of sermons and
> great addresses on the general theme of missions as to present
> the problems of practical work which are involved in the
> missionary enterprise, and to call together such persons of
> experience as could discuss them with advantage to the
> whole church.
>   The topical division comprised: (1) The missionary idea--
> asserting the claims of the Great Commission and its supreme
> aim. (2) The economics of missions, embodying organization,
> location and strength of stations, self-support and comity.
> (3) The departments of work--literacy, evangelistic, medical
> educational and industrial; work for women and for special
> classes. (4) Home administration and means of enlisting the
> church.[14]

The CIM had about twenty delegates present for the meetings,

including Mr. and Mrs. Hudson Taylor. But Taylor by now was feeble in

health and on the verge of a nervous breakdown. Nevertheless, he

---

[12]Lyall, _A Passion for the Impossible_, p. 61.

[13]Edwin M. Bliss, et al., eds., _A Report of the Ecumenical
Missionary Conference, New York, 1900_ (New York: American Tract
Society, 1900), p. 25.   [14]Ibid., p. 50.

addressed the conference several times with considerable impact.

In a moving message on "The Source of Power in Mission" the veteran missionary reminded the audience that only God's power was adequate to do God's work. Taylor warned as well, "We have given too much attention to methods and to machinery and to resources, and too little to the Source of Power, the filling with the Holy Ghost."[15]

The New York Conference was to be Hudson Taylor's last appearance at a major meeting of this kind. The news from China in April 1900 was ominous, and soon the Boxer Rebellion would break out with such tragic consequences. Yet Taylor's moving appeal for prayer for China was one of the most memorable addresses given at the conference.

Publications

Much more has been written about Hudson Taylor than he ever wrote himself. Yet Taylor did make an impact through several of his books, pamphlets, and in particular through his editorial work in China's Millions. It is amazing that he had time to write at all, given his circumstances and travel pressures. Apart from China's Spiritual Need and Claims, most of Taylor's books were produced in the latter part of his life.

Books

China's Spiritual Need and Claims was the first major writing effort by Hudson Taylor. It went through seven editions and sold thousands of copies. In the early stages of the CIM this book did as

---

[15]Ibid., p. 88.

much, if not more than any other thing to stir up interest, prayer and get recruits for China. The first edition appeared in 1866 and the last in 1877.

Hudson Taylor's autobiography was written in 1894 at the request of many who wanted a shorter version than Geraldine Guinness' earlier biography of Taylor and the CIM published in 1892. It was based on messages Taylor had given previously in conference ministry in China, and which had been printed as well in various issues of China's Millions. Since then his autobiography known as A Retrospect has gone through eighteen editions. A more recent edition, in co-operation with Bethany Fellowship, was printed and entitled under a new name, To China With Love.

Various devotional books were also written by Taylor, the most well known being Union and Communion. This devotional study, based on the Song of Solomon, probably had the best circulation of any of Taylor's writings. It was first published in 1897, and since then has gone through numerous editions, with over 50,000 copies printed. Other devotional books by Hudson Taylor were A Ribband of Blue and Separation and Service published in 1898.

China's Millions

The first edition of China's Millions appeared in 1875. This magazine, which has been the official organ of the CIM since 1875, was Taylor's primary outlet for writing to the Christian public, and it enjoyed wide circulation. The articles covered all aspects of the work in China, and went beyond just the ministries of the China Inland Mission. As an illustrated graphic, the magazine was unusual for its day in quality and standard of art work.

Taylor functioned as editor for <u>The Millions</u> and punctuated the editions with frequent editorials. Some of these editorials were printed in pamphlet form, such as <u>To Every Creature</u>, and were widely read with considerable impact.

The next chapter will deal more in detail with biographic materials concerning Taylor and the influence of his biographies over the years.

PART III

CURRENT INFLUENCE ON THE

CHRISTIAN WORLD AND

MISSIOLOGY

CHAPTER XII

IMPACT OF BIOGRAPHIC MATERIALS

Hudson Taylor by his life and ministry influenced many as has been shown already. And yet it is probably fair to say that Taylor's biographers contributed more to the influence and impact of Taylor on Christian missions than he himself did directly. For it was really Hudson Taylor's biographers who have given to the wider Christian world an enduring set of perspectives on Taylor, and displayed through their writings the model and challenge of Hudson Taylor's life. Since the publication of The Story of the China Inland Mission in 1892, CIM books have continued to touch literally thousands of lives and have contributed immeasurably to the faith missions movement and the edification of the church worldwide.

Biographies by Geraldine Guinness Taylor

In 1888 Geraldine Guinness sailed to China from England as a new missionary with the China Inland Mission. As the daughter of H. Grattan Guinness, founder of the East London Training Institute for Home and Foreign Missions, Geraldine was thoroughly acquainted with the world of missions, and in particular with Hudson Taylor and the China Inland Mission. Sensing the call of God, Geraldine Guinness went off to China expecting to spend her life there in evangelism and church planting.

However, after several years of service on the field, Hudson
Taylor and other CIM leaders recognized Geraldine Guinness's gifts in
writing and commissioned her to write a story of the CIM. Starting in
1890 Miss Guinness spent almost two years of intense research and
writing before the first volume of The Story of The China Inland Mission was finally published in 1892. The second volume was completed
in 1894.

Behind the writing of this history were several fundamental
motives which have characterized other CIM volumes as well. In the
preface of The Story of The China Inland Mission, Guinness explains:

> A three-fold purpose is before us in the publication of
> this book.
> In the first place, we desire, as a Mission, at the
> close of more than a quarter of a century's experience to
> raise a heartfelt "Ebenezer" to the glory and praise of God,
> whose faithfulness has brought us hitherto. Oh, that His grace
> toward us--so far exceeding all we could have asked or
> thought--may be the means of encouraging others to put their
> trust more and more fully under the shadow of His wings!
> Secondly, the rapid increase of our numbers on the field
> and the recent wide extension of interest in the Mission
> to Christian circles in many lands, have made some such con-
> secutive history of its past an urgently felt need. . . .
> And lastly, our hope is that through the influence of
> these pages some hearts may be awakened to a deeper sense of
> the great need of China, of the unutterable privilege of a
> life of wholehearted consecration to God, and of the
> wondrous possibilities open to a simple faith.[1]

In 1895 Geraldine Guinness married Dr. F. Howard Taylor, the
son of J. Hudson Taylor. Dr. Howard Taylor had already been at work
in China as a medical missionary with the CIM before their marriage,
and the couple continued in evangelistic work in Honan for several
years afterwards, till Dr. Taylor's ill health forced them to leave on

---

[1] Geraldine Guinness, The Story of The China Inland Mission,
(London: Morgan & Scott, 1892), 2:viii.

furlough in 1898. During this time of recuperation in Australia,
Geraldine began work on a new book about Pastor Hsi of China, and from
this point on the Taylors' lives were to take a new direction.

Growth of a Soul and Growth of a Work

From 1898 onward Howard and Geraldine Taylor had increased
contact with Hudson Taylor and cared for him personally during the last
several years of his life. With Hudson Taylor's death in 1905,
D. E. Hoste, General Director of the CIM, commissioned the Taylors to
undertake a new biography of Hudson Taylor. Taylor's early experiences
had already been published in his book, A Retrospect, and in some
detail in Geraldine's The Story of the China Inland Mission, but much
more could be told, and told differently, now that Taylor himself could
not read the record.

With characteristic thoroughness the Taylors threw themselves
into the project which would take thirteen years finally to complete.
Howard Taylor did much of the collating and classifying of materials,
and Geraldine focused on the writing itself. Few books have been
written with more intensity and prayerfulness than this two-volume
biography. Geraldine's own biographer wrote: "She communed with God
over every day's work, often over each sentence, sometimes over the
very words. She knew that without Christ she could do nothing. So she
received the book from Him, but it was not an easy process."[2]

However, the Taylors' own desire for perfection and thoroughness also created some difficulties for the CIM, anxious to publish

---

[2]Joy Guinness, Mrs. Howard Taylor: Her Web of Time
(London: China Inland Mission, 1949), p. 197.

the works. Finally, the first volume entitled Hudson Taylor in Early
Years was released in 1911. The sequel, Hudson Taylor and the China
Inland Mission, was published in 1918. The subtitles of the volumes,
Growth of a Soul and Growth of a Work of God, reveal the devotional
thrust of the biographers.

The new biography met with immediate acceptance, and by 1929
50,000 volumes had been sold of the two-volume work.[3] Over the next
several years sales increased, with approximately 100,000 volumes having
been published. This two-volume set was also translated into French and
had wide circulation.

Hudson Taylor's Spiritual Secret

As time went on the CIM saw the need for a smaller presentation
of Hudson Taylor's life and requested the Taylors to prepare a suitable
condensation of the larger work. In 1932 Hudson Taylor's Spiritual
Secret was released to meet that need.

This highly readable biography has gone through innumerable
editions and several translations--including Chinese, Japanese, German
and Spanish. The British edition by CIM, known as Faith's Venture,
has gone over 50,000 copies. In North America Hudson Taylor's Spiritual
Secret is now handled by Moody Press, and over 210,325 copies had been
sold as of February 1983.

J. Hudson Taylor: God's Man in China

As the CIM-OMF approached its centenary year since the founding
of the Mission by Hudson Taylor in 1865, a decision was made to release

---

[3]Broomhall, The Man Who Believed God, p. vii.

an abridged version of the standard two-volume biography of Hudson

Taylor. Phyllis Thompson, an accomplished author and editor, and member

of the OMF in Great Britain, was commissioned to undertake the abridg-

ment. Thus in 1965 this new biography was released as part of the

Tyndale Series by Moody Press. It has gone through several editions,

with over 40,000 volumes printed. The British edition, known simply as

Biography of J. Hudson Taylor, has sold close to 50,000 copies.

In addition, Phyllis Thompson wrote a special biography of

Hudson Taylor geared to young people. God's Venturer first appeared

in 1954 and sold over 35,000 copies.

Miscellaneous Works

Over the years a total of twenty books flowed from the pen of

Mrs. Howard Taylor. A number of these works became best sellers and

are still in circulation today. Of special significance are Behind

The Ranges, the story of J. O. Fraser; The Triumph of John and Betty

Stam; and Borden of Yale. Although the subjects for these other works

were varied, yet they focused on people related to the China Inland

Mission, and obviously helped to convey something of the ethos and con-

victions of Hudson Taylor and the Mission to thousands of readers.

Biography by Marshall Broomhall

In 1929 Marshall Broomhall, a nephew to Hudson Taylor and Home

Secretary for the CIM in Great Britain, published a new treatment of

Hudson Taylor's life called The Man Who Believed God. Although bio-

graphical details are given in Broomhall's book, yet his main effort was

in trying to identify the key qualities of Taylor's life as a man of

God and mission leader. The Man Who Believed God has gone through twenty-three reprints and sold over 80,000 copies.

Broomhall was also a prolific writer like Geraldine Taylor and
authored some thirty-one books. Some of Broomhall's works were
scholarly treatments of China and related issues. But Broomhall as
well contributed significantly to the influence of Hudson Taylor on
the Christian public, and his biography of Taylor in particular has had
considerable impact since its first release.

Biography by J. C. Pollock

J. C. Pollock is an ordained minister in the Church of England,
and in recent years has become a writer as well, with an emphasis on
Christian biography. In 1962 Pollock published a new work on Hudson
Taylor entitled Hudson Taylor and Maria. The original edition was
published by McGraw-Hill and later picked up by Zondervan Press.

Pollock in his new biography wanted to show what he felt were
neglected or distorted dimensions of Hudson Taylor. Pollock explained
in the preface of Hudson Taylor and Maria:

> James Hudson Taylor influenced millions. His fame still
> commands wide respect in Europe, America and Asia; he is of
> that select company who belong to all mankind. Notwithstanding,
> his stature is recognized only by the discerning. This is
> curious, for the two-volume official Life published after his
> death in 1905 remains a spiritual classic to be placed on the
> same shelf as Pilgrim's Progress.[4]

Pollock went on to state, however, that the Taylors in writing
their two-volume biography were products of the day, and also were
inhibited in their expression. Pollock went on to assert that:

---

[4]John C. Pollock, Hudson Taylor and Maria: Pioneers in China
(New York: McGraw-Hill, Inc., 1962; reprint ed., Grand Rapids:
Zondervan Publishing House, 1976), p. 10.

Dr. and Mrs. Howard Taylor collaborated in rather an
unusual manner. After researching together, Howard drew up
a factual "gist of the narrative"; his wife Geraldine then
moulded this into the text that was printed, and the book
in its final form is impregnated with her personality. Unfortunately, in addition to expunging, or at least severely
censoring her father-in-law's sense of humor, she suppressed
one complete love affair and half of another, as well as
incidents which to her generation may have seemed derogatory
or too private.[5]

John Pollock in his new biography sought to insert warmth and

humanness into Taylor's life and see the ". . . revered father figure

dissolved into a most lovable young man with a strong sense of fun."[6]

Since the first publication Hudson Taylor and Maria has gone through

several editions, with almost 40,000 copies sold.

Biography by A. J. Broomhall

In 1981 the Overseas Missionary Fellowship, in cooperation

with Hodder and Stoughton, launched a new series on Hudson Taylor,

which undoubtedly will become the definitive biography.

Dr. A. J. Broomhall, a retired OMF missionary, has undertaken this am-

bitious project, and already three of the proposed six-volume series

have been published entitled Hudson Taylor and China's Open Century.

As to why Broomhall started this new biography on Hudson

Taylor, he remarks:

Over the years I have read and reread the Howard Taylor and
Marshall Broomhall biographies, and twenty years ago learned
from John Pollock of the existence of unused archive documents.
My own research intended for a short biography unearthed so
much of historical value and human interest that I correlated
it chronologically for use as a source book. To my surprise
Messrs. Hodder and Stoughton judged that many readers would
welcome the full story, so, with an attempt to make it
readable, here it is, an abridged but unexpurgated, unembellished
collection of facts. In order to come freshly to the subject I

---

[5]Pollock, Hudson Taylor and Maria, p. 11.   [6]Ibid., p. 11.

deliberately avoided using the classic biographies and Pollock's imaginative <u>Hudson Taylor and Maria</u>.[7]

Broomhall has sought to place Hudson Taylor within the wider setting of his time by weaving in the strands of secular history as they bear on the subject—Catholic and Protestant missions in China, Western trade and diplomacy in China, personalities involved in the unfolding drama and Hudson Taylor's own story. Furthermore, Broomhall is attempting to show Taylor as he was, with strengths and weaknesses. Dr. Broomhall concludes:

> As indicated by its subtitles 'The Growth of a Soul' and 'The Growth of a Work of God', that biography, some anthologies and other books based on them have focused on the devotional side of Hudson Taylor's life and mission. They represent the man of God. Apart from filial respect, Howard and Geraldine Taylor's generation believed in being generous, emphasising the strengths and passing over the weaknesses, so understandably few detrimental references appear in their books or remain in their archives. Hudson Taylor, however, was also thoroughly human. Feeling deeply, thinking intensely and with catholic generosity; yet dogmatic and authoritarian, he was emotionally his own greatest handicap and goad to greater endeavour.[8]

Volume one in the series entitled <u>Barbarians at the Gates</u> appeared in 1981 and 10,000 copies were published. The second volume, <u>Over The Treaty Wall</u>, was completed in 1982, with 8,000 copies published initially. Volume three, <u>If I Had a Thousand Lives</u>, was published in 1982 as well, with a first edition of 8,000 copies. The final three volumes will be published at nine-month intervals.

Impact on Bible Schools and Seminaries

Over the years biographies of Hudson Taylor have been recommended or required reading for mission classes in many Bible schools

---

[7]Broomhall, Barbarians at the Gates, Book I, p. 12.

[8]Ibid., p. 11.

and seminaries, both in North America and elsewhere. In a recent survey
of mission professors at some fifty-two Bible schools and seminaries in
the States, questions were asked regarding the use of Hudson Taylor
biographies for mission classes.

Of the fifty-two surveyed, thirty-four replies were received.
Among the responses only four professors indicated they did not require
and/or recommend any Hudson Taylor biographies for their particular
mission classes. Six professors surveyed stated that they require a
biography, and in all cases it is Hudson Taylor's Spiritual Secret.
The other twenty-six professors recommend Taylor's biographies, the
most frequently mentioned being Hudson Taylor's Spiritual Secret,
Hudson Taylor and Maria, Hudson Taylor and the China Inland Mission
(two volumes) and Hudson Taylor and China's Open Century by
A. J. Broomhall.

Impact on Missionary Motivation

It is interesting to note how frequently Hudson Taylor's
biographies are mentioned in testimonies of missionaries as a factor in
their going to the field. In an article included in the Summer 1969
edition of the Evangelical Missions Quarterly, Charles Troutman of the
Latin America Mission surveyed factors in motivating candidates to
Latin America. The survey included 253 missionaries who had just
recently reached the field. Of the total who replied, 120 were men
and 133 were women. The missionaries surveyed represented a broad
cross-section of societies totaling thirty-nine and came from some
fifty different Bible training institutions in North America, the
majority, however, coming from Moody Bible Institute and Columbia

Bible College.

Among the several major factors influencing those new missionaries was the reading of missionary biographies. Hudson Taylor was listed as one of the most influential, along with Betty Elliott and Isobel Kuhn.[9] It has also been the experience in reviewing candidates of the CIM-OMF to note how frequently biographies of Taylor are mentioned as influential in motivating them towards missions, and in particular to the OMF.

Publication Program of the CIM-OMF

The China Inland Mission, and now the Overseas Missionary Fellowship, is unique in its overall publications program of mission books. Since the Mission's inception in 1865 till 1952 almost 300 titles were published by CIM authors. Since 1952 an additional 259 titles have been published by CIM-OMF authors.

It is difficult to estimate the impact of these books on the faith missions movement or on the Christian church. But it would be fair to say that the influence of CIM literature on the worldwide missionary cause is considerable, and the biographies of Hudson Taylor continue to challenge thousands of Christians today.

Other Media Biographies

Besides the many written biographies, the life of Hudson Taylor has been portrayed in other media as well. Several plays have been produced, along with a radio drama series done by Moody Radio.

---

[9]Evangelical Missions Information Service, Evangelical Missions Quarterly (Summer 1969), 5:209.

In 1981 Ken Anderson Films, in cooperation with the Overseas
Missionary Fellowship, released an 85-minute feature film entitled
Hudson Taylor. The film won the Christian Film Distributors Association
Award for the best missionary film of 1981, and has had widespread
recognition and response. And so the story of Hudson Taylor continues
to speak to subsequent generations in various forms.

CHAPTER XIII

UTILIZATION OF TAYLOR'S MISSIOLOGICAL

PRINCIPLES TODAY

It has been clearly demonstrated already that God used Hudson
Taylor to spearhead a new movement in pioneer outreach and launch the
faith missions movement. Scores of similar mission societies in time
came into being following the prototype of the China Inland Mission.
In this sense Hudson Taylor left an indelible imprint on world missions.
But the question arises as to what extent Taylor's missiological
principles are utilized by those in the faith missions movement today.
This chapter will attempt to delineate the key distinctives of Taylor
which are still operative in the mission societies that developed out
of this movement.

Present Influence on Faith Missions

Dr. Arthur Glasser made an astute observation in his foreword
to the centenary edition of Hudson Taylor's biography in 1965. Concerning Taylor's current influence, Glasser stated:

> Hudson Taylor is not remembered today as the strategist
> who almost singlehandedly brought about a revolutionary
> change in the missionary situation in China one hundred years
> ago, but rather as a man of God. What abide are the fragrance
> and influence of his life. For Taylor was preeminently one
> who embodied in his life a balance of qualities that marked
> him as anointed of God "above his fellows."[1]

---

[1]Taylor, God's Man in China, p. v.

While it is certainly true that Taylor's influence as a man of God outweighs other areas, yet Hudson Taylor's legacy in mission principles is still evident today in the faith missions movement. It is difficult to say with precision, however, what principles of Taylor have been incorporated by other faith missions and are still utilized today, as many other influences and factors have come into play since Hudson Taylor's period of ministry and personal influence. But there are some general principles which do remain and are operative in the faith missions movement which can be traced directly to Hudson Taylor and the China Inland Mission.

Faith and Finance

Harold Lindsell defined faith missions in the following way: "Faith missions is a term generally applied to nondenominational and interdenominational foreign missionary agencies whose governing concept is to look to God alone for financial support."[2]

Basically, faith missions have been so named because of their approach to financial support. As Harold Cook points out:

> In the missions that have followed the example of the China Inland Mission, the following principles are generally observed:
> (1) No solicitation of funds or missionaries is permitted.
> (2) No debts are allowed.
> (3) No salary is guaranteed.
> (4) Missionary candidates from any evangelical denomination are acceptable.
> (5) Evangelistic work is to have first place.[3]

---

[2]Neill, ed., _Concise Dictionary of the Christian World Mission_, p. 206.

[3]Cook, _An Introduction to the Study of Christian Missions_, p. 151.

From the financial perspective Hudson Taylor's principle of
trusting God and stepping out in faith without guarantees of salaries
or support still characterize most of the faith mission boards today.
Even though these various boards hold to the faith principle in
financing and have no "captive constituency," yet there is a considerable diversity in the application of the faith principle.

Very few societies today would still adhere to Hudson Taylor's
strict policy of nonsolicitation in the sense of not making needs
known. Most faith boards feel free to provide information, but would
restrict solicitation. This contrast is explained further by Lindsell:

> The second facet of the financial arrangement of faith
> boards is the method by which money is raised. It varies slightly
> from board to board, but ordinarily falls into one of two types.
> The first approach is used by the China Inland Mission (now
> known as Overseas Missionary Fellowship), one of the oldest of
> the faith mission boards, whose example has been followed by
> many other agencies. The China Inland Mission operates on what
> might be termed a "pure faith" basis. Its members do not make
> their financial needs known, nor do they solicit funds directly
> or indirectly. They pray in faith, expecting God to supply
> their financial and other needs. The second type of faith board
> is one which has modified one phase of the policy of the China
> Inland Mission. It does not solicit funds either, but provides
> full public information about its financial needs. Most of
> the faith boards probably fall under the latter category.
> Boards of both types usually agree that the monies which come
> in represent God's appraisal of their real needs and mark the
> limit of the agency's responsibility to its missionaries. In
> the first instance when the mission board has discharged its
> obligation by prayer, and in the second instance when the
> agency has discharged its obligation by the presentation of
> its needs and prayer, the results are left in the hands of God.[4]

Thus, although there are differences in application or inter-
pretation of faith and finance, the fundamental principle of looking

---

[4]Harr, ed., *Frontiers of the Christian World Mission
Since 1938*, p. 189.

ultimately to God rather than to an institution or denominational structure for support is still very much evident in faith boards today.
Each missionary is expected to look to God for the supply of his needs
and not to the mission board. Missionaries then receive no guaranteed
income or allowance, although many boards do set support quotas and hold
back personnel from going overseas till those quotas are met by various
supporting churches and individuals. The CIM-OMF would differ in this
respect, having a pooling system versus an individual support plan.
However, Hudson Taylor's basic principle of looking to God first and
not to man is still reflected in the faith missions movement today.

Interdenominational Membership

An area in which Hudson Taylor pioneered was the concept of a
transdenominational mission society open to men and women from any
orthodox and evangelical church. This nonsectarian approach to missions
still characterizes the faith missions movement in principle. Membership and support come from different evangelical denominations as well
as from independent churches. Faith boards usually hold to a doctrinal
statement that covers the fundamentals of the faith but omits some of
the controversial points that have separated denominations. This
pattern can be traced directly back to Hudson Taylor, as Harold Cook
points out:

> The faith mission movement owes its origin to the vision
> and zeal of J. Hudson Taylor. In setting up the China Inland
> Mission (1865) he had no thought of being antidenominational.
> He was merely shouldering a burden for the evangelization of
> inland China that no denomination of that time was willing to
> undertake. He could not count on either personnel or support
> through regular denominational channels. Thus his dependence
> had to be on God's moving the hearts of individual Christians,
> and his ecumenical spirit welcomed workers from all evangelical

groups.[5]

Although most faith boards are theoretically nondenominational or interdenominational, in practice this theory is not always carried out consistently. Some faith boards have so defined their doctrinal statements and recruiting practices as to virtually eliminate membership from certain evangelical segments of the church. Harold Lindsell, in analyzing faith missions in recent years comments:

> Thus a particular board may refuse to accept a confirmed Pentecostalist who believes that speaking in tongues is a necessary evidence of a conversion experience. Some boards with a Calvinistic emphasis may refuse to accept staunch Arminians who believe that a man may fall from grace subsequent to his conversion experience. Often the decision is made on the basis of the individual and an appraisal of his willingness to maintain doctrinal harmony of a station when he is likely to be in disagreement with other workers about certain doctrinal beliefs. But faith boards do not normally inquire into the doctrinal persuasions of those who support the work financially.

Use of Laymen and Women

Hudson Taylor felt strongly that credentials for missionary service involved more than academic degrees. In opening the door to missionary service for nonordained men and those with less formal education, he pioneered a new concept in nineteenth century missions. This pattern to a certain degree has continued in the faith missions movement and can be seen in many faith boards today.

However, in recent years with the proliferation of Bible and mission training programs, coupled with a growing demand for higher

---

[5]Harold R. Cook, Highlights of Christian Mission (Chicago: Moody Press, 1967), p. 66.

[6]Harr, Frontiers of the Christian World Mission Since 1938, p. 193.

qualifications in cross-cultural missionaries, the trend is definitely towards more thorough preparation. But as Herbert Kane points out, "In spite of the changes that have come about, the Bible colleges continue to provide the lion's share of candidates for the faith missions."[7]

A quick glance at the ratio of women to men in missions will also confirm the fact that Hudson Taylor's principle of using women in pioneer work is still very much in evidence today. It is estimated that in missionary societies women outnumber men three to two and constitute the majority. Approximately one-third of the missionary constituency would be single women. As Kane aptly put it, "When all is said and done, single women missionaries have a strategic role to play on the mission field, and with few exceptions they play it well."[8]

Miscellaneous Principles

There are other missiological distinctives of Hudson Taylor which still influence faith missions in the twentieth century. Taylor's stress on the priority of the unreached has marked the great majority of boards. In terms of mission strategy there would be some application particularly as seen in the evangelism-in-depth programs and, more currently, in the frontier missions movement.

The China Inland Mission pioneered missionary children's education on the field, and this has become the pattern for most boards today. Stress on the identification and the building of a culturally relevant, indigenous church are principles all boards espouse. In the

---

[7]J. H. Kane, _Understanding Christian Missions_ (Grand Rapids: Baker Book House, 1974), p. 161.   [8]Ibid., p. 62.

one area of headquarters on the field, very few boards have adopted this principle. And, finally, Hudson Taylor's pattern of disseminating missionary information and recruitment appeals finds echoes in many groups still today.

Overseas Missionary Fellowship

The mission known today as the Overseas Missionary Fellowship is the successor to the China Inland Mission. When the name was changed in 1964 at a special council of all directors of the Mission, a revised constitution was also issued in keeping with the new developments in their sphere of operation in East Asia. However, as the Principles and Practice of the OMF declare: "This reconstitution. . . involves no change in the basic principles of the original document." [9]

The distinctives of the early CIM are still very much a part of the present OMF. No basic changes have taken place other than administrative adaptations due to changing circumstances. The financial policy of Hudson Taylor remains the same, along with other principles of interdenominational membership, headquarters on the field, and an emphasis on identification and a simple lifestyle. In terms of the priority of the unreached, the overarching aims of the OMF are described in the Mission Handbook as:

> The aim of the Fellowship is the speediest possible evangelization of East Asia's Millions. The vast majority of the unreached people of the world live in Asia. The goal of our work therefore is:
> The widest possible dissemination of the Christian gospel by every means.
> The most thorough possible teaching of Christian disciples.

---

[9]Overseas Missionary Fellowship, Principles and Practice, p. 1.

148

The speediest possible planting of new congregations.
The greatest possible perfecting of established
congregations, that is, briefly--preaching, teaching,
planting and perfecting.[10]

The Fellowship, however, recognizes that the command of Christ
to preach the gospel to every creature is given to the whole church of
God. Missionary activity therefore is to stimulate and supplement,
not substitute for the witness of the local church. The overall aim
of the Fellowship may therefore be further defined as: "A church in
every community, and therefore the gospel to every creature."[11]

Thus in policy and ethos the CIM still lives very much today
in its successor, the Overseas Missionary Fellowship. Pollock in his
foreword to Hudson Taylor and Maria summarizes well the line of
continuity when he says:

The China Inland Mission has had an influence far beyond
its immediate spheres of operation. This influence has
stemmed partly from a high standard of leadership and the
qualities demanded of those who serve, partly from its
literature, but largely because it has always sought, in
financial affairs as much as in activities, to depend on that
element of simple faith in God which is so foreign to so much
of this modern age, but is a sure foundation of all lasting
Christian endeavor.
These characteristics derive directly from the adventures
and discernments of Hudson Taylor himself. To most missions
a founder is nothing but a name, and, perhaps, a whiskered
photograph on the office wall. The spirit and personality
of Taylor permeate the CIM still. Through all the changes
and developments of an up-to-date, go-ahead Mission they have
not lost what he gave them.[12]

[10]Overseas Missionary Fellowship, Handbook, p. 4.

[11]Ibid., p. 4.

[12]Pollock, Hudson Taylor and Maria, p. 10.

CHAPTER XIV

KEY FACTORS IN CURRENT INFLUENCE

Thousands of gifted, committed missionaries have gone out to the vast unreached areas of the world over the last one hundred years. And yet, interestingly, very few names are known today apart from a select handful of unique pioneers. Hudson Taylor has become one of those household·names in Christian circles and continues to attract attention. Taylor's biographies sell well and his name frequently occurs as a reference in mission discussions. At present there appears even to be a resurgence of interest in Taylor's life, ministry and accomplishments.

But what accounts for this almost perennial attraction to the life of Hudson Taylor? Why does this missionary among so many from the past have such appeal to the Christian church today? This chapter will seek to examine several of the key factors which possibly account for the current influence of Hudson Taylor.

A Balance of Qualities

Arthur Glasser once wrote: "J. Hudson Taylor belongs to the whole Christian church. Down through the years his life, labors and worldwide spiritual impact have inspired thousands who have 'imitated his faith' and discovered for themselves the utter faithfulness of his

149

Master, the Lord Jesus Christ."[1] In analyzing those qualities in

Hudson Taylor which made him so effective, Glasser spoke of "a balance

of qualities that marked him as anointed by God 'above his fellows.'"[2]

Glasser goes on to point out four significant qualities.

The first quality noted is that Hudson Taylor was ambitious

without being proud. There is no doubt that Taylor's vision was

enormous, and his designs or plans stretched far beyond most of his

contemporaries. His ambition was to see all of China evangelized by

whatever means possible, and nothing could cloud that vision.

> Men strongly differed with him and harshly criticized his
> methods. They thought the vast range of his vision almost
> arrogant. They were repelled by the tenacity with which he
> pursued his objectives. They could not help having misgivings
> over the drive that took him to the forefront of all mis-
> sionary work in his day. Such consuming ambition![3]

Hudson Taylor saw much of his dream for China realized. God

largely granted him his heart's desire. And yet, as Glasser comments:

> Taylor's sharpest critics again and again went out of their
> way to comment on his humility: "How lowly he remained in his
> own eyes. God was able to take that beloved man and make him
> a prince among all the missionaries of the Victorian era"--
> this from Eugene Stock, the able leader of the Church Missionary
> Society.[4]

Thus Hudson Taylor was able to keep in balance his largeness of

vision with genuine humility which attracted rather than repelled men.

A visitor to Taylor's house in England in 1876, at a time when Taylor

was invalided because of a back injury, made the observation:

> I strongly suspect that, by his unconscious influence,
> Mr. Hudson Taylor did more than any other man of his day to
> compel Christian people to revise their ideas of greatness.
> He never used his position as Director of the Mission to

---

[1]Taylor, God's Man in China, p. v.

[2]Ibid., p. v.   [3]Ibid., p. v.   [5]Ibid., p. v.

purchase for himself the least advantage or ease. However
hard his lot might be in China, every missionary knew that
Hudson Taylor had suffered in the same way, and was ready
to do so again. No man could suspect, at anytime, that while
he himself was bearing the cross, his leader under more
favorable circumstances, was shirking it.[5]

The second of Taylor's outstanding qualities which contributed
to his effectiveness and winsomeness was that he was catholic without
being superficial. Obviously, the needs of China and his own China
Inland Mission demanded great attention and time. Taylor was a skillful
organizer and administrator, and the growth of the Mission reflects that
ability.

And yet Taylor had a large heart that could reach out beyond
the immediate and show genuine concern for other areas and other
ministries. Taylor apparently was not afflicted with that insidious
disease of organizational jealousy, which unfortunately characterizes
many Christian organizations today:

> No downgrading of other missions. No criticism of those
> whom he couldn't surpass. Hudson Taylor stood against the
> divisive spirit that tolerates duplication and competition.
> His call to his peers was that they trust one another more,
> and fear one another less.[6]

The third quality noted by Glasser is that Hudson Taylor was
biblical without being bigoted. Taylor was primarily a man of the Book
and it showed in every dimension of his life. Robert Wilder in
reference to Taylor's ministry at Northfield in 1888 recalled:

> The students loved to hear him expound the Word of God.
> He was a master of his Bible, and his sympathy and natural-
> ness attracted men to him. His addresses were so much
> appreciated that Mr. Moody had to announce extra meetings
> to be held in the afternoon, as many of the students were
> anxious to hear more from the veteran missionary. . . . Eternity
> alone can reveal the results of that life and the effect of his

---

[5]Ibid., p. 246.   [6]Ibid., p. vi.

work on our student movement.[7]

Taylor was a man of strong convictions and strong loyalties to Christ and His Word. At times his hermeneutics might be questioned, but not his devotion to biblical principle. Glasser observed:

> Hudson Taylor's loyalty to Christ and His Word made him aggressive in his defense of the faith. Arthur T. Pierson spoke of his "strange wonderment" at the readiness of clergymen to make concessions to the rationalistic enemies of supernaturalism. Taylor often used the illustration of the Russian who tossed out his children one by one to the pursuing hungry wolves in order that he himself might escape their violence. "Why appease the clamor of these critics," he would thunder, "by tossing out vital truths of the faith? Don't have less faith in God than you have in man!"[8]

And yet Taylor was remarkably free of bigotry. He recognized that within the Body of Christ there was an essential unity which must be maintained in spite of certain doctrinal differences. Breaking fellowship with other believers over minor matters was no small matter to Taylor. The founder of the China Inland Mission was a convinced Baptist himself, but felt that in the ministry of the CIM the core of essential truths which united it was more important than the minor issues which could divide it. And thus "he organized the CIM so that its doctrinal grid would be forthrightly evangelical, yet free from both obscurantism and dogmatism on minor matters." The Mission's survival after 118 years of potential conflict speak well for the wisdom of Taylor in this area.

The last quality Dr. Glasser observed in Taylor which contributed to his appeal was that Hudson Taylor was charismatic without

---

[7]Basil Miller, J. Hudson Taylor: For God and China (Grand Rapids: Zondervan Publishers, 1948), p. 118.

[8]Taylor, God's Man in China, p. vi.   [9]Ibid., p. vi.

being selfish. Taylor was able to command loyalty through his warmth,
sensitivity and servant spirit to others. One of his greatest gifts
was the ability to create strong ties of mutual esteem and affection
which over the years attracted so many people to him.

It is true that at times Taylor was authoritarian and even
dogmatic over strategies or solutions. Taylor had his share of mis-
understandings with fellow workers. But when he challenged people, they
responded and followed because of his compelling gift of leadership.
He never asked others to do what he was not willing to undertake
himself.

And yet, as Dr. Glasser points out, this gift was never abused:

> Taylor was charismatic, but without any trace of self-
> centeredness. No misusing of God's gracious gift to him. No
> empire building, no pyramiding of financial or personal power.
> No suppression of fellow Christians. Hudson Taylor sank all
> personal interests into a consuming desire to serve, no matter
> how humble or difficult the service.[10]

Even at the age of sixty-two with poor health, Taylor undertook an
arduous trip from Shanghai to Sian in North China in order to deal with
a critical situation that could have resulted in the loss of fifty CIM
associate members. The journey covered several thousand miles and took
nine months of unbelievable hardships in travel. Taylor's daughter-in-
law tried to dissuade him by saying, "It may cost you your life, dear
father." To which Taylor replied, "Yes, but we ought to lay down our
lives for the brethren."[11] No wonder Hudson Taylor inspired
followers.

---

[10]Ibid., p. vii.

[11]Guinness, Her Web of Time, p. 118.

154

Pioneer Model

Since the early 1970s a new thrust in missions has been developing and is now generally called the Frontier Missions Movement. One of the key proponents of the Frontier Movement is Dr. Ralph Winter, formerly of the School of World Mission at Fuller Theological Seminary, and now director of the U.S. Center for World Missions in Pasadena.

In analyzing the eras of missions history, Dr. Winter has used Hudson Taylor as a pioneer model and initiator of a new era in missions. Following the first era in modern missions launched by William Carey, Hudson Taylor is next portrayed by Winter as initiator of the second era, with a new focus on the unreached, or the "inlands" of the world.

Drawing parallels to today, Winter and others see Taylor as a pioneer model and one worthy to be emulated. It is interesting to note that two chapters are given to articles by Hudson Taylor in Perspectives of the World Christian Movement: A Reader, edited by Ralph Winter and Steven Hawthorne. This reader is being widely read by students and others. But it is Taylor's vision for the unreached and his commitment to reach them that are frequently being used as a model to challenge new missionaries to move out to the frontiers and the unreached of our day.

Spiritual Life

The fact that Moody Press alone from 1959 to 1983 sold over 210,000 copies of Hudson Taylor's Spiritual Secret is evidence of the spiritual qualities in Hudson Taylor which continue to attract Christians today. Perhaps in more than any other way, Taylor's life and experiences have provided a stimulus to faith for thousands of believers

around the world. Robert Wilder, intimately connected with the beginnings of the Student Volunteer Movement, expressed this quality in
Hudson Taylor when he said, ". . . he not only made the needs of the
mission field very real; he showed us the possibilities of the
Christian life."[12]

Hudson Taylor himself longed to show that God is faithful and
will never fail those who trust Him wholly. Thus a recurring theme
throughout Taylor's life is the faithfulness of God. Faith was a continual subject of Hudson Taylor's editorials, letters and messages;
but the emphasis was not so much on faith as on the object of our faith,
the living God. Taylor not only talked about faith and the faithfulness of God, his experiences and those of the China Inland Mission were
living examples that it is possible to move men, through God, by prayer
alone. Thus this ability to stimulate faith accounts in large measure
for Taylor's ongoing influence.

In 1965 Bishop Frank Houghton, retired General Director of the
CIM, wrote a special anthology for the centenary year of the Mission
entitled The Fire Burns On. Houghton sought to identify those marks of
Hudson Taylor and the early China Inland Mission which caught the attention and impressed the Christian public then. Included among these
qualities were love, faith, prayer, sacrifice and hope. In the words of
Mrs. Howard Taylor, what characterized Taylor and his "motley crew"
the most was "reality, simplicity and intensity."[13]

---

[12]Taylor, God's Man in China, p. 296.

[13]Houghton, The Fire Burns On, p. 12.

Hudson Taylor sought not only to plant the church in China, but also to stimulate Christians at large to the possibilities of the Christian life. This universal dimension of Taylor's ministry accounts considerably for his impact still today. It is very evident that God has used Hudson Taylor to demonstrate how God's strength is made perfect in weakness. Taylor himself recognized this when he said, "All God's giants have been weak men, who did great things for God because they reckoned on His being with them." This testimony to the sufficiency of God for life's greatest needs puts Taylor in an enduring role to minister to Christians anytime and anywhere.

PART IV

LESSONS, PERSPECTIVES AND GUIDELINES

FOR MISSIOLOGY TODAY

CHAPTER XV

RECRUITMENT PATTERNS

It is easy to slip into sentimental hagiography when writing

about people of the past. Obviously, Hudson Taylor was a product of

his Victorian era and reflected perspectives and certain limitations

of that time. And yet there is much of abiding validity to world

missions today from the life and ministry of this man. As a Southern

Baptist missionary in China testified, even in 1894, regarding Taylor's

contribution to his own ministry:

> I remember one day while walking in a Chinese city with
> Dr. Hudson Taylor. As we walked along he said in his quiet
> way: "Brother Bryan, the learning of the Chinese language is
> less than half of what we have to learn. There are the
> people whom we must learn." And he went on to say that not-
> withstanding the fact that they knew so little about the Lord
> Jesus Christ, it was best not to stand and harangue them for
> an hour or two. But to take a central thought and for fifteen
> or twenty minutes to carry that thought to their hearts. Those
> things were worth more than gold to me. We young missionaries
> can sit at the feet of these older missionaries and know things
> in a few hours that took years for them to learn.[1]

In this final section the focus will be on the lessons, perspectives

and guidelines derived from the life and work of Hudson Taylor for

missions today.

One of the major lessons coming from Taylor's ministry relates

to the area of motivating and mobilizing the church for missions.

---

[1]Max Wood Moorhead, ed., The Student Missionary Enterprise:
Addresses and Discussions of the Second International Convention of
the Student Volunteer Movement, February 28–March 4, 1894 (Boston:
Press of T. O. Metcalf & Co., 1894), p. 232.

The historical record clearly demonstrates that over the centuries the biggest problem in missions is not so much getting the nonChristian to listen to the gospel as mobilizing the church to proclaim the gospel. Even today in spite of great advancements in world missions a shortage of mission personnel is evident. Yet Hudson Taylor was able to recruit directly or indirectly some 800 missionaries into the China Inland Mission and channel many others into other societies. The question naturally arises as to what were the human factors that made him so successful in mobilizing people for the cause of missions. The following is an attempt to analyze some of those factors and to suggest principles for application to missions today.

Dealing with First Causes

At an early stage in the CIM Hudson Taylor learned a crucial principle in recruitment. As he records in his autobiography, A Retrospect: "In the study of that Divine Word I learned that to obtain successful laborers, not elaborate appeals for help, but first earnest prayer to God to thrust forth laborers, and second, the deepening of the spiritual life of the church so that men should be unable to stay at home were what was needed."[2]

Through the years of Taylor's leadership of the CIM special appeals for new workers were made periodically. But each special appeal grew out of a strong sense of spiritual burden and a confidence springing from faith that God in answer to prayer would provide the laborers. And the appeals themselves were not so much a cry for personnel as a plea for prayer that God would raise them up.

---

[2]Taylor, A Retrospect, p. 117.

Hudson Taylor recognized that unless new workers are God-sent they hinder rather than help the work of missions. He saw that earnest prayer to the Lord of the Harvest must precede plans, programs and any other promotional efforts in recruitment. As Taylor put it, "Let us go to the right quarter for our missionaries. Not to the plough or to the anvil, not to the university or the forum, but to the great Head of the church."[3] Hudson Taylor was confident that the Lord of the Harvest could be depended upon to select and to send the right men and women.

The call for the One Hundred in 1887 is a good example of Taylor's priority of prayer in recruitment. He testified later how God led and worked:

> It is not lost time to wait upon God. May I refer to a small gathering of about a dozen men [the first China Council of the CIM] in which I was permitted to take part some years ago, in November 1886. We in the China Inland Mission were feeling greatly the need of Divine guidance in the matter of organization on the field, and in the matter of reinforcement, and we came together before our Conference to spend eight days in united waiting upon God--four alternate days being days of fasting as well as prayer. This was November, 1886, when we gathered together; we were led to pray for 100 missionaries to be sent out by our English board in the year 1887. . . . What was the result? God sent us offers of service from over 600 men and women. . . and it proved that at the end of the year exactly 100 had gone.[4]

There is no doubt that the growth of the CIM and the amazing response in offers of missionary service stemmed primarily from the fact that Taylor and his colleagues prayed first and recruited second. This is a vital lesson which mission boards and the sending churches

---

[3]Johnston, Report of the Missionary Conference, London, 1888, 1:17.

[4]Bliss, et al, eds., A Report of the Ecumenical Missionary Conference, New York, 1900, p. 88.

today need to learn afresh.

Use of Creative Facts

Hudson Taylor prayed for workers. But he also made every
effort to present the needs and opportunities of China to the Christian
public in an intelligent and compelling way. Taylor was an idealist,
but he was also a pragmatist. He knew well that information prayerfully presented was just as important in motivating the church for
missions. As John R. Mott shared at the 1910 Student Volunteer
Movement Convention: "It was when Hudson Taylor mastered the facts, in
order to write for a certain publication about the needs of China
that he began to pray for twenty-four workers and did not cease praying
until he had those workers, the germ of a mission that now includes
a thousand workers in China."[5]

It is instructive, however, to see the way in which Taylor
presented the facts of China and directed the appeals for additional
workers. Even a brief perusal of copies of China's Millions, along
with special recruitment publications like China's Spiritual Need and
Claims, demonstrate the many creative efforts to inform and motivate.
Given the information lag which most Westerners had about China in the
nineteenth century, it is impressive to see the way Taylor drew
constant parallels with the familiar world of Europe to teach the
unfamiliar world of China. Taylor included bar graphs, diagrams and
statistical charts, among other graphic materials, to communicate the

[5]Fennell P. Turner, ed., Students and the Present Missionary
Crisis: Addresses of the Sixth International Convention of the Student
Volunteer Movement for Foreign Missions, Rochester, New York, 1910
(New York: Student Volunteer Movement for Foreign Missions, 1910),
p. 171.

true situation. The use of poetry, vivid accounts of missionary work, principles and pithy sayings, such as "One million per month die without Christ in China" all combined to communicate a compelling message. Special articles for children were written as well and included as regular features in the Mission's magazine, China's Millions.

Marshall Broomhall recalls some of the ways Taylor was able to communicate through the use of creative facts:

> He never wearied of arraying facts before the Christian public, and of getting to close quarters with his hearers or readers in their application. He knew how to appeal to the imagination, how to speak to the conscience, and how to move the heart also. He himself was so dominated by creative convictions that he could make them contagious.[6]

Hudson Taylor was convinced that "missionary intelligence is essential to missionary effort, and the more definite the information the better."[7] He was seldom before an audience without the use of visual aids such as maps or charts. Taylor's sermons, while biblical were also replete with anecdotes and stories in order to paint visual pictures for his hearers, and thus to reinforce the message.

Missions today have more tools than ever before to present the facts of mission. Every effort should be made to assure that these tools are used in creative ways, but at the same time with accuracy and integrity. Facts alone, however, will not be enough. Facts must be coupled with genuine experience, biblical principles and communicated in prayer and dependence upon God.

---

[6]Broomhall, The Man Who Believed God, p. 205.

[7]Ibid., p. 204.

Task Before Agency

Another important lesson that can be derived from Hudson
Taylor's success in recruitment for missions lies in the area of
focus. Although Taylor naturally spoke in reference to the CIM, yet
his major focus in presentation was on the task first and not on the
organization. Taylor himself said, "We do not need to say much
about the CIM. Let people see God working, let God be glorified,
let believers be made holier, happier, brought nearer to Him, and they
will not need to be asked to help."[8]

For Taylor, the critical issue was not the survival or reputation of the mission agency, but rather the needs and opportunities in
China. Even the missionary was to have second place to the task
itself, that is, the evangelization of China. Thus his constant stress
was on the task before the church, and he exerted every effort to communicate the vision of a million people dying each month in China
without Christ and hope.

As a result, the attention of the Christian public was turned
to China itself and secondarily to the CIM as an agency. Taylor was
convinced that the important issue was the reaching of China, and
whatever agency could help in achieving that primary goal had his
support and blessing.

Hudson Taylor in his focus on the task over the agency provides
a needed perspective for mission societies today. At a time when resources in finance or personnel may be limited, the danger of
competition and organizational promotion is very real. What a helpful

---

[8]Taylor, God's Man in China, p. 176.

reminder then to keep in focus the fact that if the task is of God, it is his responsibility to provide the workers and the resources to finish the task. As the agency maintains a servant spirit and sees itself as a means to an end, then God will faithfully sustain its cause without the help of gimmicks and manipulation.

Self-disclosure

Hudson Taylor was an effective communicator and speaker. But his appeal to people was not due just to his facility with words. In fact, Taylor's platform presentation, comparatively speaking, did not have the force and strength of many of his contemporaries. However, within Taylor was the capacity for self-disclosure and honesty which enabled his audience to identify with him and establish rapport. Broomhall described this quality in the following way:

> But a large measure of his power and appeal lay, not in the facts alone, but in his own impressive personality. He had a way, not given to every man, of baring his own heart. He could speak with freedom of the most intimate experiences, of his trials and sorrows, his bereavements and anxieties, his times of want and times of deliverance, of his spiritual failures and spiritual triumphs in Christ. He took hearers by the heart, he admitted his readers into his most sacred confidences, and men were drawn to him and knit to him in the deepest things. This is apparent on almost every page of A Retrospect, and on many a page of China's Millions when he was editor.[9]

When Hudson Taylor spoke with students and potential candidates for missionary service, he not only challenged them with needs, opportunities and ideals, but also helped them to see the enablement God could provide to fulfill each divine assignment. Taylor spoke frequently from his experience of growth, failure and development which

---

[9]Broomhall, The Man Who Believed God, p. 206.

lent credibility to his message and motivated others to go and do
likewise.

In surveying several of Hudson Taylor's messages at the 1894
Student Volunteer Convention in Detroit, the above pattern of sensitive
self-disclosure can be readily seen. Taylor used statements such as,
"I look back upon the time when my precious children had to be sent
away from the country; when I was just crushed and sick and alone in
the house in which loving little footsteps had been the great joy of
one's life."[10] Or again frank admissions such as, "It was many a year
after I was a Christian before the Holy Ghost was more than an influence to me."[11] And, "Now there has been much failure on my part
and on the part of those who worked with me, but there has been no
failure on the Lord's part, none at all. That little work began in
a very small and tiny way, and the Lord picked the least man perhaps
physically and intellectually and in every other way that He could lay
His hand on when He called me for that purpose. . . ."[12]

Taylor's willingness to show his inner person in a candid way
evidently gave a winsomeness and appeal to him as a speaker and made
him extremely approachable as a person. Thus Hudson Taylor carried
authenticity in his manner, and this in turn facilitated his ability to
attract and recruit new workers. Or as another speaker at the same
Detroit convention put it as he referred to Taylor, "We know how we
were all touched this morning by the words of Dr. Taylor of the China

---

[10]Moorehead, ed., Student Missionary Enterprise, p. 149.

[11]Ibid., p. 149.

[12]Ibid., p. 34.

Inland Mission. Why? Simply because he quickened our spiritual lives."[13]

Passion

A grand vision had captured Hudson Taylor, and his passion to see the vision turned to reality was evident in all he wrote and spoke. This passion generated tremendous energy and vitality which attracted the interest of thousands. Taylor was able to communicate an excitement which then solicited the excitement and commitment of others.

Although there was warmth and a positive approach to Taylor's presentations, yet they also were filled with great intensity of purpose. This sense of earnestness was contagious. Behind Hudson Taylor there was a strong sense of responsibility which drove him in passion to obey and recruit others as well in Christ's cause for China. An illustration of this can be seen in an extract from the appeal for The Seventy in 1882:

> Souls on every hand are perishing for lack of knowledge; more than a thousand every hour are passing away into death and darkness. . . provinces in China compare in area with kingdoms in Europe, and average between ten and twenty millions in population. One province has no missionary; one has only one, an unmarried missionary; in each of two other provinces there is only one missionary and his wife resident, and none are sufficiently supplied with labourers. Can we leave matters thus without incurring the sin of blood-guiltiness?[14]

On another occasion Taylor pleaded:

> And the gospel must be preached to these people in a very short time, for they are passing away. Every day, every day; oh, how they sweep over! Your great cataract Niagara seems to me to teach us a lesson and to afford us an example.

---

[13]Ibid., p. 197.

[14]Taylor, Growth of a Work of God, p. 360.

How the water pours over and over ceaselessly by day and by night, over that great cataract! There is a great Niagara of souls passing into the dark in China. Every day, every week, every month they are passing away--a million a month in China are dying without God. And what a wonderful difference there is in dying with God, dying with God as a Saviour, and dying without God.[15]

The implications for missionary recruitment from this point are obvious. Cold facts of need are not enough to motivate the church to action. Even facts spoken with enthusiasm are insufficient to adequately challenge today's generation. Rather, effective recruitment must be the overflow of a deep, genuine commitment to a biblical task which results in a sense of urgency and passion to enlist others.

The Missionary Call

To Hudson Taylor the missionary call, although profound in implications, was never seen as unduly mystical or complicated. His ability, thus, to communicate the call of God to missions in moving yet practical ways accounted in part for his effectiveness as a missionary communicator and recruiter.

Taylor never lowered the standards of a missionary or soft-pedaled the demands, but he did stress the responsibility of every believer to seriously consider the call to foreign service and felt that many more could go than were actually going. To Hudson Taylor, the commands of Scripture regarding the Great Commission were obvious, and the real question for each believer was to weigh up whether or not his general circumstances, health and abilities would allow him to serve elsewhere. Because Taylor also minimized the need for extensive academic preparation, many more applicants responded to the CIM than to

---

[15]Moorhead, ed., The Student Missionary Enterprise, p. 48.

most other mission societies of the day. In other words, Taylor
challenged any believer of reasonable health and qualifications to
justify why he or she should not go, in light of the commands of
Scripture and the unmet needs in the world.

Furthermore, there was no conflict in Taylor's mind either in
using prayerful reason and the intellect in determining the if and
where of a missionary call. The point of greatest need should probably
be the place of service. At the same time, he did not demean the need
for assurance of God's call and adequate preparation. But for Taylor,
the overwhelming need demanded a response from Christ's disciples, and
no one was exempt from that responsibility.

However, in emphasizing the need to go into all the world
regardless of obstacles, Taylor tended to downplay the role and responsibility of the local church to select and to send. That is, Hudson
Taylor placed a strong emphasis on the personal call and the mission
agencies' responsibility to screen without adequate regard to the
sending church. Perhaps in light of Taylor's earlier experience with
indifference or inability of the church to respond to China's claims,
the stress on an individualistic call is understandable.

Hudson Taylor's practical approach to the missionary call has
lessons for the church today, especially in view of Taylor's very real
success in recruitment. He never formulized the call of God, nor did
he ignore it and use need alone to persuade. The commands of Scripture,
the needs of the world and the general circumstances of the believer
were all significant factors to be carefully and prayerfully considered.

But through it all, Taylor's burning convictions and heartcry for the
lost are the greatest challenge to the missionary recruiter today.

> Oh, think not so much of China's needs and claims as of
> Christ's needs and claims. When on earth His voice was heard.
> That voice is silent. He wants your voice to go. When on
> earth His eyes wept over the perishing. Those eyes weep no
> more; He wants your eyes to weep over the perishing. Christ
> has need of you, dear brothers; Christ has need of you, dear
> sisters. To many of you here it may be His call, His claim,
> His duty will require you to work at home, and it is very
> blessed to work at home if He wants you to. But there are
> many others, I am quite sure, who, if they are abiding in
> Christ, will not abide in the United States. The Lord has
> need of lights in the darkness. And oh, how great the
> darkness is![16]

---

[16]Moorhead, ed., The Student Missionary Enterprise, p. 48.

CHAPTER XVI

ABIDING PRINCIPLES FOR MISSIONS

The writer of the book of Hebrews exhorts us to "Remember those who led you, who spoke the word of God to you; and considering the result of their conduct, imitate their faith" (Hebrews 13:7). Although the context is different, yet there is legitimacy in applying the exhortation in principle to missions today to remember and imitate the faith of early missionary pioneers who were greatly used of God. And there is certainly much that modern missions can learn afresh with great profit from the life and ministry of Hudson Taylor.

Although mission technology today is perhaps more sophisticated than in Hudson Taylor's era, yet there are essential principles to the success of missions which Taylor's life clearly model. This chapter will focus on four basic principles which apply to the missionary task in any age.

Vision

The dictionary defines vision as intelligent foresight. This quality was certainly possessed by Hudson Taylor and set him apart from many of his peers. Taylor had the capacity to visualize the future and then take the needed steps to meet the claims and opportunities of the future. As Dr. Henry Frost, the first CIM Home Director in North America, described this quality in Taylor: "Mr. Taylor was a man who

169

always had a morrow in his heart. He was born of the Spirit with his face forward and belonged to God's advance guard."[1]

But Hudson Taylor's vision is something that should be more than simply admired. Rather, this pioneer missionary, with his ability to see the world's needs and respond accordingly, is a dimension that must be a part of missions today. From Taylor's vision there are important lessons for this generation's missionaries as well.

Claim of the Unreached

There were many voices clamoring for Hudson Taylor's attention. But there was one voice which he could not ignore, that is, the voice of the unreached. When Taylor first went to China in 1853 as a young missionary, a deep concern for the lost and unreached was obviously a part of his life. But during his first furlough as Taylor studied the wider dimensions of China's needs, the realization came that not just part but all of China must be reached.

As Taylor gazed at the map of China before him, he could not escape from the awesome responsibility of some eleven provinces in China with a total population of 200 million without one single Protestant missionary. Added to that were the other seven underworked provinces along with the neglected dependencies of Manchuria, Mongolia, Ili, Tsinghai and Tibet—and the total picture was one of gigantic need.

The cumulative effect of the statistics of China drove Taylor to action finally and launched a new mission. But the vision was born out of a careful analysis of actual needs, and once seen irrevocably

---

[1]Henry W. Frost, Unpublished manuscript, "Years That Are Past," (Princeton, N.J., 1932), p. 201.

committed Taylor to responsible obedience. This vision and sense of responsibility he sought to share with others also:

> It is the prayerful consideration of these facts, and the deepening realisation of China's awful destitution of all that can make man truly happy, that constrains the writer to lay its claims as a heavy burden upon the hearts of those who have experienced the power of the blood of Christ; and to seek, first from the Lord, and then from His people, the men and means to carry the Gospel into every part of this benighted land.[2]

Taylor went on to show that awareness of the facts was not enough. He pleaded as well that "The claims of an empire like this should surely be not only admitted, but realised."[3]

During the next twenty-five years of ministry, Hudson Taylor saw much of his vision for China realized. By 1890 most of the provinces had been occupied with mission stations and churches established and evangelism being carried out throughout inland China. And yet Taylor could not rest with only part of the vision realized. In 1890 at the Shanghai Missionary Conference he presented a bold new plan for the completion of the task. Taylor suggested a scheme to reach every family throughout China over a period of three years. The plan called for an additional 1,000 missionaries. Even though the number seemed considerable, if not impossible, yet to a visionary like Taylor committed to a God-given task, the 1,000 seemed only reasonable.

Taylor's plan itself might be questioned from the viewpoint of church-planting strategy, but his vision for the unreached masses is a fresh challenge to the world of missions today. Dr. Ralph Winter expressed a similar application when he said of Taylor, "Even his early

---

[2]Taylor, China's Spiritual Need and Claims, p. 48.

[3]Ibid., p. 47.

anti-church-planting missionary strategy was breathtakingly erroneous by today's church-planting standards. Yet God strangely honored him, because his gaze was fixed upon the world's least-reached peoples."[4]

Hudson Taylor could not rest knowing that a large proportion of the world's population was falling into a Christless eternity. He stated at a student conference: "God forbid that our hearts should be satisfied while any part of the world is without Christ. . . Christ loved all the world. Our blessed Saviour could not rest in heaven itself and leave you and me out. He must come to seek us."[5] Taylor today would challenge all of us anew to a bold new vision of the task to reach the unreached regardless of the cost.

Trying the Impossible

If ever a mission door seemed closed in the early 1850s it was the door to inland China. Even later in 1865 when the CIM was formed the walls to the interior seemed just as impregnable. Taylor was told to wait, both as to aggressive attempts to evangelize the inland provinces and until the resources were in hand. But Hudson Taylor found himself ". . . still challenged by the open Bible, the ever-accusing map. The Master has said nothing about politics or finance in his Great Commission."[6]

And so Taylor set out to do the impossible, not because he felt adequate, but because God commanded. As Taylor wrote to a friend:

---

[4]Winter and Hawthorne, eds., The World Christian Movement, p. 172.

[5]Moorhead, ed., Student Missionary Enterprise, p. 46.

[6]Broomhall, God's Man in China, p. 160.

"When will it dawn on the Lord's people that His command to preach the Gospel to every creature was not intended for the wastepaper basket?"[7] Obstacles to man were not obstacles to God, and Hudson Taylor's vision of the unreached drove him on to believe God for miracles and opened doors. Even trying was not seen as good enough. On this line Taylor challenged missionary colleagues at the 1890 Shanghai Missionary Conference:

> It seems to me that we want to ask more seriously than I have done in bygone days, what is really the will and command of our blessed Lord, and to set about obeying Him, not merely attempting to obey. I do not know that we are told anywhere in the Bible to try to do anything.[8]

Taylor went on to say:

> And if as an act of obedience we were to determine that every district, every town, every village, every hamlet in this land should hear the Gospel, and that speedily; and we were to set about doing it, I believe that the Spirit would come down with such mighty power that we should find loaves and fishes springing up on every hand.[9]

Hudson Taylor had a passion for the impossible. In fact, on one occasion Taylor said that there were three stages in doing the will of God. First it was impossible, then difficult, and then done. The great challenge of Taylor is to our feeble faith and dimmed vision. Too many Christians today are discouraged by the problems of how to evangelize in the secularized culture around them or in the so-called closed or resistant countries where Islam or Communism have raised their various curtains. But the claim of the unreached must not go unanswered, and the problems or obstacles must not be allowed to weaken our vision of the Great Commission. If it is true that over half the

---

[7]Broomhall, The Man Who Believed God, p. 203.

[8]Taylor, Shanghai Conference, 1890, p. 6.   Ibid., p. 6.

world today is still outside the reach of normal evangelistic efforts by
the church, and some 16,750 people groups are still without adequate
witness, then no less vision is required by us than it was by Hudson
Taylor. Taylor would remind us again that the impossible is possible
if God is in it.

Faith

The present challenge of the unreached world in size and com-
lexity is probably greater than in the days of Hudson Taylor. Yet
Taylor's life and the accomplishments of the China Inland Mission are
a constant reminder of God's sufficiency and faithfulness to His people
and work in any age. Taylor in a unique way was forced to trust God
and lean upon Him for exceptional needs. But towards the end of his
life, Hudson Taylor could still testify:

> I have sometimes met people who said: "Trusting God is a
> beautiful theory; but it won't work." Well, thank God, it
> has worked and it does work. I remember a dear friend, an
> aged minister in London, who said to me in the year 1866:
> "You are making a great mistake in going to China with no
> organization behind you. We live in a busy world, and you
> will all be forgotten, and the Mission won't live seven
> years." That [said Hudson Taylor] was the prophecy of this
> good man--and a wise one too. But he was mistaken.[10]

Proving God

Taylor came to realize that vision alone is not adequate to complete a God-given task. Only faith and dependence upon the living God
will see the task accomplished. Someone has said that the mission
fields of the world are strewn with the wreckage of good intentions.
Over and over again Taylor came to realize the peril of this statement,

---

[10]Broomhall, Our Seal, p. 3.

but he went on to become a case study for others to see God's ability to supply each need. Marshall Broomhall, in a book witnessing to the faithfulness of God to the CIM, wrote in 1933 the following summary:

> The China Inland Mission from its beginning has staked its very existence upon the faithfulness of God. His promises have been taken at their face value. They have been put to every conceivable test. They have been proved by many painful emergencies, they have been sifted as wheat by extraordinary and imperative demands, they have passed triumphantly through the crucible of war, they have been weighed in the gold and silver scales of exchange, and they have never failed.[11]

When Taylor was called to form the China Inland Mission he sensed that God was entering into a sacred covenant with him. Hudson Taylor's reticence to move forward and launch a mission previously had been due to his inability to face the consequences and demands of such a step. But at Brighton Beach on June 25, 1865, Taylor came to see that the consequences of any act of obedience to God must ultimately be God's alone. If God called, then He must enable and He must provide. Taylor recorded years later the moment of insight which led to rest and faith in the plan of God:

> All at once came the thought--if you are simply obeying the LORD, all the responsibility will rest on Him, not on you! What a relief!! Well, I cried to God--you shall be responsible for them and for me too! I had never before identified [myself] with the band--or yielded to be their leader. Then and there prayed for 24 men for inland China. . . . There the Lord conquered my unbelief, and surrendered myself to God for this service. I told Him that all the responsibility as to issues and consequences must rest with Him.[12]

Over the years Hudson Taylor proved the promises of God. He believed in God's promises and was prepared to step out and risk life

---

[11]Ibid., p. 4.

[12]Broomhall, If I Had a Thousand Lives, Book III; p. 45.

itself. God was to him a "living bright reality," and this sense of confidence in the faithfulness of God enabled and ennobled his ministry. Taylor once wrote to prospective new candidates this expression of his confidence in God:

> The Word has said: 'Seek first the kingdom of God and His righteousness, and all these things [food and raiment] shall be added unto you.' If anyone did not believe that God spoke the truth, it would be better for him not to go to China to propagate the faith. If he did believe it, surely the promise sufficed. Again, 'No good thing will he withhold from them that walk uprightly.' If anyone did not mean to walk uprightly he had better stay at home. If he did mean to walk uprightly, he had all he needed in the shape of a guarantee fund. God owns all the silver and gold in the world, and the cattle on a thousand hills. We need not be vegetarians![13]

The application to missions today is obvious and needed. No work of God will be left to flounder for lack of resources if their trust is in God. In the face of restricted economies, run-away inflation in some countries or financial upheavals in all, faith missions must be true to their calling and name. The temptation to look first to endowments, institutions or individuals for support rather than to God is ever present.

Out of the crucible of experience Hudson Taylor came to prove God is a faithful Heavenly Father. God was his Father, and prayer to Taylor was "a word to the Big Heart from the little one."[14] "I do not believe," he wrote, "that our Heavenly Father will ever forget His children. I am a very poor father, but it is not my habit to forget my children. God is a very, very good Father. It is not His habit to forget His children."[15] This quiet attitude of trust in the character

---

[13]Broomhall, The Man Who Believed God, p. 107.

[14]Ibid., p. 180.   [15]Ibid., p. 139.

and promises of God needs to be reflected in the present missionary
enterprise as well. "God's work done in God's way will never lack
God's supply" is a motto not just for the CIM, but is applicable to
any mission agency today.

The Faith/Rest Principle

In 1888 at the Centenary Conference of Protestant Missions in
London Hudson Taylor shared a revealing personal insight. Before this
august assembly of missionary leaders and churchmen Taylor confessed:

> I fully believe, my Christian friends, in the words of the
> last speaker, that we must not lower the standard of mis-
> sionary service. I think we want to raise it immensely.
> I believe in the Holy Ghost, and in the power of the Holy
> Ghost. We have been too much satisfied with men who have
> not had to a large degree the power of the Holy Ghost. I
> speak for myself. Many years I spent in spiritual work in
> China, in which I was oftener hungry than well-fed, oftener
> thirsty than overflowing. We want a higher standard of
> Holy Ghost power in all our missionary servants if they are
> to do the work of the church effectually.[16]

Hudson Taylor came to realize through personal struggle that
missionary life, or even the Christian life, cannot be lived without
total dependence upon the indwelling Christ. In 1869 Taylor evidently
sank into a black despair and, uncharacteristically, recorded nothing
in his daily journal for seven weeks. A letter from a fellow missionary, however, threw a flood of light into his soul. This
experience dramatically changed Hudson Taylor's life and ministry,
and was one from which he never apparently looked back.

Mrs. Howard Taylor in an abbreviated biography of Hudson Taylor

---

[16]Johnston, ed., Report of the Missionary Conference, London,
1888, 2:16.

described the incident as "the exchanged life".[17] From this point on

Hudson Taylor's ministry seemed to be an overflow from an inner suf-

ficiency which enabled him to face unbelievable tests and demands in

the years ahead. The following is taken from a letter written to Amelia

Broomhall, Taylor's sister, and illustrates the impact of this spiritual

experience on Hudson Taylor's subsequent life and ministry.

> As to work--mine was never so plentiful, so responsible, or
> so difficult, but the weight and strain are all gone. The
> last month or more has been, perhaps, the happiest of my life,
> and I long to tell you a little of what the Lord has done for
> my soul. . . .
> My mind has been exercised for six or eight months past,
> feeling the need personally and for our Mission of more
> holiness, life, power in our souls. But personal need stood
> first and was greatest. I felt the ingratitude, the
> danger, the sin of not living nearer to God. I prayed, agonized,
> fasted, strove, made resolutions, read the Word more diligently,
> sought more time for meditation--but all without avail. . . .
> When my agony of soul was at its height, a sentence from
> a letter from dear McCarthy was used to remove the scales from
> my eyes, and the Spirit of God revealed to me the truth of
> our oneness with Jesus as I had never known it before.
> McCarthy, who had been much exercised by the same sense of
> failure but saw the light before I did, wrote:
> "But how to get faith strengthened? Not by striving
> after faith, but by resting on the Faithful One."
> As I read, I saw it all! "If we believe not, He abideth
> faithful." I looked to Jesus and saw (and when I saw, oh, how
> joy flowed!) that He had said, "I will never leave thee."
> "Ah, there is rest!" I thought, "I have striven in vain
> to rest in Him. I'll strive no more. For has not He promised
> to abide with me--never to leave me, never forsake me?"[18]

Through this experience Taylor came to see that the enablement

for life and ministry comes through abiding in the all-sufficient

Christ. He went on to say to his sister Amelia:

> Oh, my dear sister, it is a wonderful thing to be really

---

[17]Dr. and Mrs. Howard Taylor, Hudson Taylor's Spiritual Secret
(Philadelphia: China Inland Mission, 1932), p. 112-115.

[18]Ibid., p. 112.

one with a risen and exalted Saviour, to be a member of
Christ! Think what it involves. Can Christ be rich and I
poor? Can your right hand be rich and your left poor?
Or your head well-fed while your body starves?[19]

Taylor went on to summarize the implications of this new sense

of identification with Christ:

> The sweetest part. . . is the rest which full identifi-
> cation with Christ brings. I am no longer anxious about
> anything, as I realize this: for He, I know, is able to
> carry out His will, and His will is mine. It makes no
> matter where He places me, or how. That is rather for Him
> to consider than for me, for in the easiest position He
> must give me His grace, and in the most difficult His grace
> is sufficient. It little matters to my servant whether I
> send him to buy a few cash worth of things, or the most
> expensive articles. In either case he looks to me for the
> money and brings me his purchases. So, if God should place
> me in serious perplexity, must He not give me much guidance:
> of great pressure and trial, much strength? No fear that
> his resources will prove unequal to the emergency. And
> His resources are mine, for He is mine, and is with me,
> and dwells in me.[20]

It is easy in the study of mission theory to lose sight of the

absolute necessity for effectiveness or fruitfulness to flow out of

abiding in Christ rather than simply correct strategy. The spiritual

life of the missionary can never be separated from the task of missions,

and is done so only at the loss of power and abiding results.

Hudson Taylor invested much of his time as a mission leader

seeking to cultivate the spiritual effectiveness of his fellow workers

and the supporting constituency at home as well. Obviously there were

many other important dimensions to the missionary task, but nothing as

fundamental. The abiding lesson of Hudson Taylor to missions today is

that planning, organization, sophisticated equipment and anything else

---

[19]Ibid., p. 112.   [20]Ibid., p. 116.

cannot substitute ultimately for the power of Christ. For Christ Himself said, "Without me, you can do nothing."

Commitment

Among the many important principles that emerge from Taylor's life and ministry, none is more applicable to our day than that of commitment. Hudson Taylor reminds the would-be missionary or the Christian anywhere, "There are not two Christs--an easy-going one for easy-going Christians, and a suffering, toiling one for exceptional believers. There is only one Christ. Are you willing to abide in Him and thus to bear much fruit?"[21] Commitment clearly marked the ministry of Hudson Taylor and represents a challenge to the world of missions today.

Obedience to the Great Commission

Hudson Taylor was convinced that the Great Commission is not an option to be considered, but a command to be obeyed. The great passion of his life was to fulfill the Commission in China and mobilize the church at home to greater commitment to this task as well. All of Taylor's energies were thrown into the evangelization of China, and he expected no less of his fellow workers. Something of Hudson Taylor's commitment to the Great Commission can be seen in the following extract from a letter to prospective candidates:

> One-third of the human family is in China, needing the
> Gospel. Twelve millions there are passing beyond the reach
> of that Gospel every year. If you want hard work and little
> appreciation; if you are prepared to take joyfully the

---

[21]J. Theodore Miller, Great Missionaries to China (Grand Rapids: Zondervan Publishers, 1947), p. 112.

spoiling of your goods, and seal your testimony, if need be, with your blood; if you can pity and love the Chinese, you may count on a harvest of souls now and a crown of glory hereafter 'that fadeth not away'; and on the Master's 'Well done.'[22]

The obstacles to the fulfilling of the missionary task were considerable, but Taylor and his band of missionaries would not be stopped. To read the account of frequent riots, angry mobs, physical privations, hazardous trips, loss of children, and other trials is to marvel at the commitment of these pioneer missionaries. Most went to China realizing that the likelihood of early death was highly probable. In actuality the average life expectancy of expatriates in China during the mid-1800s was only seven years.[23] Yet Taylor himself said, "If I had a thousand lives China should claim every one. No, not China, but Christ. Can we do too much for Him? Can we do enough for such a Savior?"[24]

The evangelization of inland China meant inescapable hardship, sacrifice and even suffering for the sake of the gospel. And yet it was a price those early pioneers were willing to pay. Beside his dying daughter in an old, ruined temple, Hudson Taylor expressed something of the realities of self-sacrifice when he wrote to Mr. Berger in England:

It was no vain nor unintelligent act when, knowing this land, its people and its climate, I laid my wife and children with myself on the altar for this service. And He whom so unworthily, yet in simplicity and godly sincerity, we are and have been seeking to serve--and with some measure of success--He has not

---

[22]Taylor, God's Man in China, p. 242.

[23]Broomhall, If I Had a Thousand Lives, Book III, p. 193.

[24]Broomhall, The Man Who Believed God, p. 98.

left us now.[25]

Taylor's persistence, even through great illnesses and handicaps is amazing. There were times when Hudson Taylor had to direct the affairs of the Mission from a bed as an invalid. When Taylor returned to England in October 1874 he was threatened with the possibility of never being able to walk again due to a spine injury from a fall. For months he was forced to lie flat on his back, only able to move from side to side by means of a rope fixed over his head. Yet even in this state of weakness he continued to pray and plan for developments in China. With a map of China fixed at the foot of his bed, Taylor prayed passionately, and out of these conditions launched his appeal for eighteen new workers to enter the nine still unoccupied provinces. Hudson Taylor would never allow adversity alone to paralyze his activities.

Taylor realized that half-hearted efforts would not achieve the evangelization of China. This total commitment was reflected in many areas, including his willingness to endure loneliness and long periods of separation from his wife and children at times for the sake of the work. This to Taylor was the most difficult sacrifice of all to make. It is interesting to note, however, that half of Taylor's surviving children returned to China as CIM missionaries; and through the years four generations of Taylor's children have subsequently served as foreign missionaries.

The commitment of Taylor was reflected in his self-discipline and devotional habits as well. Because of the peculiar circumstances of life in China and the lack of privacy, Hudson Taylor was forced to

---

[25]Taylor, <u>Hudson Taylor's Spirtual Secret</u>, p. 96.

rise at 3:00 a.m. or so and spend an hour or two in Bible study and prayer. The impact of this regular feeding on God's Word was evident in his writings, messages and personal interaction with all he met.

Suffering for the Gospel

The political context in nineteenth century China was always volatile. Relations with the West were frequently strained, with the result that anti-foreign sentiment ran high at times. Missionaries were caught in the political squeeze and occasionally found themselves the victims of mob violence.

Hudson Taylor and the China Inland Mission took their share of suffering in this respect as well. But unlike many Westerners, and even some mission societies, the CIM adopted a policy of refusing claims for reparations or looking to diplomatic sources for protection. This policy was incorporated into the Principles and Practice of the Mission which stated:

> Too great caution cannot be exercised by all missionaries residing or journeying inland to avoid difficulties and complications with the people, and especially with the authorities. Every member must fully understand that he goes out depending for help and protection on the Living God, and not relying on an arm of flesh. While availing himself of any privileges offered by his own or the Chinese government, he must make no demands for help or protection, though in emergencies he may need to ask for it as a favour. Appeals to Consuls or to the Chinese officials to procure the punishment of offenders or to demand the vindication of real or supposed rights, or indemnification for losses are to be avoided. . . .
> Those engaged in the Lord's work should be prepared to "take joyfully the spoiling of their goods" and to "rejoice that they are counted worthy to suffer shame for His name." Let them be imbued with the same spirit of Ezra (Ezra viii. 21-23).[26]

---

[26] China Inland Mission, Instructions for Probationers and Members, pp. 7-8.

At times this policy was to be sorely tested, especially during
the Boxer Rebellion in 1900, when loss to the Mission was extreme. And
yet this attitude of patient suffering for the gospel's sake was to
help the Mission immeasurably to gain a hearing for the gospel and ease
some of the hostile feelings towards foreigners in China.

The example of Taylor and the CIM has application for missionary work in any setting, especially in today's uncertain world.
Robert E. Speer of the Student Volunteer Movement, using the model of
the CIM, drives home this important principle for any mission society
today as well.

> The missionary has his rights, and there are times when
> he may justly claim them, when it would be wrong for him to
> waive them and obtusely permit injustice and crime. . . .
> On the other hand, there are times when he must surrender
> them in the interest of his mission. The right principle is
> that he should lay aside all selfishness, all desire for mere
> personal protection. . . and do what will be best for Christ's
> church. . . .
> The Principles and Practice of the missionary society
> which has the largest number of missionaries in China, sets forth
> a view with which, theoretically at least, I think the great
> majority of all Protestant missionaries agree, and which I am
> quite sure defines their actual practice.[27]

Simple Lifestyle

For Hudson Taylor and the early missionaries of the CIM, the
adoption of a simple lifestyle was not just a natural consequence of
living in primitive conditions, but the outcome as well of a conscious
choice to identify with the Chinese for the sake of the gospel. This
involved a commitment on the part of each worker to live on a standard
which would not create any unnecessary stumbling blocks or barriers

---

[27]Robert E. Speer, Missionary Principles and Practice
(New York: Fleming H. Revell Co., 1902), p. 105.

in communication and ministry. Taylor once challenged new workers:

> Let there be no reservation. Give yourself up wholly and
> fully to Him whose you are and whom you wish to serve in this
> work, and there can be no disappointment. But once let the
> question arise, 'Are we called to give up this or that?';
> once admit the thought, 'I did not expect such and such incon-
> venience or privation', and your service will cease to be
> that free and happy one which is most conducive to efficiency
> and success. . . . Let us in everything not sinful become
> Chinese that we may by all means 'save some'.[28]

There is a great deal of talk these days regarding the need for
a simple lifestyle for Christians. Mission societies, however, need to
seriously address this question as well. Obviously, supporting a missionary in an inflationary environment demands careful adjustment to
meet the financial realities. But there is also the ever present danger
that support levels may provide a standard of living which not only
taxes the resources of sending churches, but places barriers between
missionaries and their host culture. If faith boards do not prayerfully monitor their commitment to a simple lifestyle, they may price
themselves out of the missionary support market. Hudson Taylor's
example and commitment are worthy of closer examination.

Prayer

One of the most valuable lessons coming from the life and work
of Hudson Taylor is the reminder that mission advance is inextricably
linked with prayer. Gratefully, technological developments have provided many helpful tools for missionary work, along with organizational
structures that greatly facilitate the recruitment, sending, maintenance and support of mission personnel. But Hudson Taylor would remind

---

[28]Taylor, God's Man in China, p. 187.

the missionary enterprise that tools and organizations can never sub-

stitute for God's power which comes alone in answer to prayer.

In answer to prayer Taylor saw hundreds of missionaries sent to

the field. In answer to prayer the CIM saw God's supply for the support

of each member. As people prayed, doors to closed provinces opened,

Chinese became responsive and the church grew and spread across the

land.

Towards the end of his career Hudson Taylor was greatly con-

cerned for the total evangelization of China. Just prior to the 1890

Shanghai General Missionary Conference, and burdened for the addition

of new workers to complete the task, he wrote to his wife:

> We must get on to a higher plane of thought altogether,
> and of prayer, if we are to walk worthy of God and deal in
> any sensible way with the world's crying need. Let us ask in
> faith for such workers for every department as shall be fit
> and able to deal worthily with their work at home, in America,
> in China, and for such an enduement of power as shall make
> the feeblest mighty and the strong as the angels (messengers)
> of God.[29]

Taylor felt strongly that every effort should be extended both

organizationally and methodologically to facilitate missions. He was

not a man given to wishful dreaming or armchair pietism. But at the

same time, Hudson Taylor realized that dependence upon God in prayer

was the ultimate way for doing spiritual work. He wrote in 1891 the

following, which highlights the place of prayer in missions:

> Few of us perhaps are satisfied with the results of
> our work, and some may think that if we had more, or more
> costly machinery we should do better. But oh, I feel that
> it is Divine power we want and not machinery! If the
> tens or hundreds we now reach daily are not being won to
> Christ, where would be the gain in machinery that would

---

[29]Taylor, Growth of a Work of God, p. 467.

enable us to reach double the number? Should we not do well,
rather, to suspend our present operations and give ourselves
to humiliation and prayer, for nothing less than to be filled
with the Spirit and made channels through which He shall
work with resistless power?[30]

Those who knew Hudson Taylor recognized him as a man of prayer.

Frequent mention was made of Taylor in messages at Student Volunteer

Movement conferences and other places. The following reference illus-

trates Taylor's reputation in this area:

> I know it is said of Hudson Taylor--and I doubt not it is
> true--that he himself has said, that in all his busy life,
> with multitudinous demands upon him, he has done one thing,
> day by day; he has made place and way for prayer, believing
> that if he did this, the other things would be taken care of,
> that the will of God would be done, and that He would be
> glorified, so far as the effort of Hudson Taylor himself
> was concerned.[31]

Taylor's final challenge to the missionary enterprise is simple

but profound. God's work must be done in God's way. John R. Mott

summarized Hudson Taylor's advice to missionaries of any age when he

said: "In this connection there are some words by Hudson Taylor which

every volunteer should ponder again and again: 'How important,

therefore, to learn before leaving England to move men, through God,

by prayer alone.'"[32]

---

[30]Taylor, <u>God's Man in China</u>, p. 325.

[31]Student Volunteer Missionary Union, <u>Students and the
Missionary Problem: Addresses Delivered at the International
Missionary Conference, London, 1900</u> (London: Student Volunteer
Missionary Union, 1900), p. 141.

[32]Mott, <u>Addresses and Papers of John R. Mott</u>, 1:359.

CHAPTER XVII

SUMMARY

Volumes of books and scores of articles have been written about Hudson Taylor, and the tremendous influence of his work worldwide is difficult to calculate. This project has been an attempt to trace something of that influence on the faith missions movement in particular and the wider world of missions in general. Obviously there were many forces at work which contributed to the faith missions movement as a whole; and although Taylor's contribution was significant, it was not the only element in the movement's formation and spread. Hudson Taylor was one of many instruments used by God to stir the church in unprecedented ways towards world evangelism in the nineteenth century. But in the alchemy of events Hudson Taylor came on the scene at a very strategic time, and his vision and pattern of outreach contributed greatly to the spread of a movement which would mushroom into a missionary force of thousands.

Impact

It has been shown clearly that the work of Hudson Taylor through the China Inland Mission had a key role in stimulating world evangelism. The CIM became a model or pattern for other missions in China as well as in creating new faith mission boards in similar molds elsewhere. Although the CIM was not, strictly speaking, the first of

188

its kind, yet because of its size and visibility it became a pattern which directly or indirectly influenced other groups and became the basic proto-type of the movement.

The impact of Taylor on other faith missions can be seen, both in terms of organizational structures and policies. The very term faith mission derives its meaning from the financial pattern first shown by the China Inland Mission. The stamp of Hudson Taylor has been in-delibly left on every mission society which calls itself a faith board.

Providentially, the rise of the Student Volunteer Movement co-incided with the emergence of the faith missions movement. Men like Hudson Taylor presented an impressive model of faith, love and com-mitment and helped immensely to stimulate recruitment for the mission fields of the world. Taylor's impact alone on key leaders in the SVM, such as John R. Mott, Robert Speer and Robert Wilder, had widespread and long-lasting effects.

As iron sharpens iron, so Hudson Taylor was both influenced and had an influence on scores of other church and mission leaders. His par-ticipation in major mission conferences in China and in the West created an impact not only on individuals but also on organizations and strate-gies. It is difficult to assess the extent of his influence, but obviously in the interchange of ideas Taylor's innovative concepts, pas-sionate commitment to world evangelism, and his gracious, godly spirit left deep impressions on many.

Perhaps more than in any other area, God has used Hudson Taylor and his colleagues in the CIM as a stimulus to faith. In ways both big and small the CIM became a living object lesson to many, demonstrating in unmistakable terms that God can be trusted. Over and over again

God was put to the test and found totally faithful to His promises.
The testimony of the CIM to God's ability and willingness to supply
needs in answer to prayer alone has become a blessing to untold thousands
of Christians over the years. Perhaps in the wider picture of God's plan
this has been the greatest function of the Mission.

His Legacy

It is instructive to note that although scores of worthy pioneer
missionaries have come and gone, few have had the ongoing biographical
attention of Hudson Taylor. Obviously there have been worthy qualities in Taylor which have attracted the attention of various writers
and motivated them to share his life and work with others. Some of
these biographies have become classics, and will in all likelihood
continue to be read by future generations of Christians.

Hudson Taylor has indirectly bestowed a legacy through the
volumes written about him. To read his life closely is to realize he
was as human, fallible and subject to error as any other mortal. And
yet the attraction seems to be in the way in which God brought strength
out of weakness and demonstrated His power in a frail but yielded
vessel.

There is always the danger in a biography of biased selectivity,
which either makes the character into an unrealistic saint, or debunks
the heroes of the past to make them as much like us as possible.
The legacy of Hudson Taylor, however, is that in spite of the weaknesses,
failures and puny resources of men, both spiritually and intellectually,
God is able to use people like us to achieve remarkable deeds. Taylor
sought to give credit and glory to God for all that was achieved in

China through the CIM. Even so, the reality of Hudson Taylor's spiritual life, his humility and integrity have given the credibility to his ministry and made it such a worthy model to be remembered and imitated.

His Challenge

Decades have passed since Hudson Taylor lived and worked for China. Yet the seeds he sowed in that land are still bearing fruit today. Likewise, the life of Hudson Taylor. still has many challenges for the church of Christ and to missionary outreach.

Taylor has reminded us that ultimately missions is God's work and can only be done in God's way. Faith is not an option, but the basis by which God's power and resources are made available to His servants. Our generation needs to hear afresh that God does answer prayer, and He is utterly faithful to His Word. Faith missions must never forget the very nature of their unique calling to a life of faith, and beware of putting their trust in respectable reputations, institutions or promotional sophistication to maintain their cause.

Hudson Taylor's life is also a continual challenge for us to look out on the "inlands" of our world where multitudes are still untouched or neglected. The priority of the unreached must never be forgotten. At the same time, he would remind missionaries of our day that obedience to reaching the lost will inevitably involve a cost. There are no easy shortcuts to planting the church; and suffering, self-sacrifice and a servant spirit will be prerequisite to fruitfulness and success in any setting.

The final challenge of Hudson Taylor is to believe God: to believe that God can do the impossible, and that obstacles and barriers

are not insurmountable if we simply follow in obedience to His will. It
is our responsibility to believe and obey and God's responsibility to
provide and guide. Hudson Taylor's life and ministry are a vivid
demonstration of that unchanging principle.

BIBLIOGRAPHY

Africa Industrial Mission (SIM International). "Minutes of the Organizational Meeting." Toronto, 27 May 1898.

Armerding, Hudson Taylor. "China Inland Mission and Some Aspects of Its Work." Ph.D. dissertation, University of Chicago, 1948.

Beach, Harlan P. A Geography and Atlas of Protestant Missions. 2 vols. New York: Student Volunteer Movement for Foreign Missions, 1901.

Beach, Harlan P. and St. John, Burton, eds. World Statistics of Christian Missions. New York: The Committee of Reference and Counsel of the Foreign Missions Conference of North America, 1916.

Beaver, R. Pierce. Ecumenical Beginnings in Protestant World Missions: A History of Comity. New York: Thomas Nelson & Sons, 1962.

Bingham, Rowland V. "Death of Rev. J. Hudson Taylor." The Missionary Witness, September 1905, pp. 129-132.

_____. "A Story of Beginnings: Dr. Andrew Murray and the South Africa General Mission." The Missionary Witness, September 1915, p. 271.

Bliss, Edwin M. A Concise History of Missions. New York: Fleming H. Revell Co., 1897.

_____, ed. The Encyclopedia of Missions. 2 vols. New York: Funk & Wagnalls, 1891.

_____, et al., eds. A Report of the Ecumenical Missionary Conference, New York, 1900. New York: American Tract Society, 1900.

Broomhall, A. J. Hudson Taylor and China's Open Century, Book I: Barbarians at the Gates. London: Hodder and Stoughton and the Overseas Missionary Fellowship, 1981.

_____. Hudson Taylor and China's Open Century, Book II: Over the Treaty Wall. London: Hodder and Stoughton and the Overseas Missionary Fellowship, 1982.

_____. Hudson Taylor and China's Open Century, Book III: If I Had A Thousand Lives. London: Hodder and Stoughton and the Overseas Missionary Fellowship, 1982.

Broomhall, Marshall. The Jubilee Story of the China Inland Mission. Shanghai: China Inland Mission, 1915.

_____. The Man Who Believed God: The Story of Hudson Taylor. London: China Inland Mission, 1929; reprint ed., London: Overseas Missionary Fellowship, 1971.

_____. Our Seal, London: China Inland Mission, 1933.

_____, ed. In Memoriam--J. Hudson Taylor. London: Morgan & Scott Ltd., 1905.

China and the Gospel: An Illustrated Report of the CIM. Shanghai: China Inland Mission, 1914.

"China Inland Mission." The Missionary Review 2 (March-April 1879):89.

China Mission Handbook. Shanghai: American Presbyterian Press, 1896.

China's Millions. London: Morgan & Scott, 1875-1905.

Conley, Joseph F., RBMU International. Personal letter, 7 February 1983.

Cook, Harold R. Highlights of Christian Missions. Chicago: Moody Press, 1967.

_____. An Introduction to the Study of Christian Missions. Chicago: Moody Press, 1954.

Dennis, James G.; Beach, Harlan P.; and Fahs, Charles H., eds. World Atlas of Christian Missions. New York: Student Volunteer Movement for Foreign Missions, 1911.

Dubose, Francis M., ed. Classics of Christian Missions. Nashville: Broadman Press, 1979.

Eddy, Sherwood. Pathfinders of the World Missionary Crusade. New York: Abingdon Cokesbury Press, 1945.

Frizen, Edwin L., Jr. "An Historical Study of the Interdenominational Foreign Mission Association in Relation to Evangelical Unity and Cooperation." Major Project, Trinity Evangelical Divinity School, 1981.

Frost, Henry W. "Days That Are Past." Unpublished autobiography, 1932.

Glover, Robert Hall. *The Progress of World-Wide Missions*. Introduction by Delavan L. Pierson. New York: Harper & Brothers, 1939; rev. and enl. by J. Herbert Kane, 1960.

Goddard, Burton L. gen. ed. *The Encyclopedia of Modern Christian Missions*. Camden, N.J.: Thomas Nelson & Sons, 1967.

Grubb, Norman P. *C. T. Studd: Athlete and Pioneer*. 7th ed. Grand Rapids: Zondervan Publishing House, 1946.

Guinness, Geraldine. *The Story of the China Inland Mission*. 2 vols. London: Morgan & Scott, 1892.

Guinness, Joy. *Mrs. Howard Taylor: Her Web of Time*. London: China Inland Mission, 1949.

Harr, Wilber C. *Frontiers of the Christian World Mission Since 1938*. New York: Harper & Brothers, 1962.

Houghton, Frank, comp. *The Fire Burns On: CIM Anthology, 1865-1965*. London: Overseas Missionary Fellowship, 1965.

Howard, David M. *Student Power in World Missions*. 2nd ed. Downers Grove, Il.: InterVarsity Press, 1979.

"Hudson Taylor." *Christian Herald*, July 1905, p. 604.

Hulbert, Homer B. "The China Inland Mission." *The Missionary Review* 22 (April 1889):257.

Hunter, J. H. *A Flame of Fire: The Life and Work of R. V. Bingham, D.D.* England: Hazell Watson & Viney Ltd., Aylesbury and Slough, 1961.

Instructions for Probationers and Members of the CIM. Shanghai: China Inland Mission, 1925.

Johnston, Arthur. *The Battle for World Evangelism*. Wheaton: Tyndale House Publishers, Inc., 1978.

Johnston, James, ed. *Report of the Centenary Conference on the Protestant Missions of the World*, 2 vols. New York: Fleming H. Revell, 1888.

Kane, J. Herbert. *A Concise History of the Christian World Mission: A Panoramic View of Missions from Pentecost to the Present*. Grand Rapids: Baker Book House, 1978.

_____. *Faith Mighty Faith*. New York: Interdenominational Foreign Mission Association, 1956.

_____. *Understanding Christian Missions*. Grand Rapids: Baker Book House, 1974.

Latourette, Kenneth S. A History of Christian Missions in China.
New York: MacMillan Co., 1929.

_____. A History of the Expansion of Christianity. Vols. 4, 5, 6.
New York: Harper & Brothers, 1941, 1943, 1944.

Lewis, W. J.; Barber, W. T. A.; and Hykes, J. R., eds. Records of the
General Conference of the Protestant Missionaries of China.
Shanghai: American Presbyterian Mission Press, 1890.

Lyall, Leslie T. A Passion for the Impossible. 2nd ed. London:
Overseas Missionary Fellowship, 1976.

MacGillivray, D. A Century of Protestant Missions in China, 1807-1907.
Shanghai: Presbyterian Mission Press, 1907.

Mason, Alfred DeWitt. Outlines of Missionary History. New York:
George H. Dolan Co., 1912.

Miller, Basil. J. Hudson Taylor: For God and China. Grand Rapids:
Zondervan Publishers, 1948.

Miller, J. Theodore. Great Missionaries to China. Grand Rapids:
Zondervan Publishers, 1947.

Moorhead, Max Wood, ed. The Student Missionary Enterprise: The Second
International Convention of the Student Volunteer Movement,
1894. Boston: T. O. Metcalf & Co., 1894.

Mott, John R. Addresses and Papers of John R. Mott. Vol. 1. The
Student Volunteer Movement for Foreign Missions. New York:
Association Press, 1946.

_____. The Evangelization of the World in This Generation. New
York: Student Volunteer Movement for Foreign Missions Press,
1946.

Neill, Stephen. A History of Christian Missions. Harmondsworth,
Middlesex, England: Penguin Books, Ltd., 1964.

Neill, Stephen; Anderson, Gerald H.; and Goodwin, John, eds. Concise
Dictionary of the Christian World Mission. Nashville: Abingdon
Press, 1971.

Occasional Papers of the China Inland Mission. 4 vols. London: China
Inland Mission, 1865-1875.

Oldham, J. H. "Romance and Reality in Missionary Work: Fifty Years of
the China Inland Mission." The International Review of
Missions 4 (July 1915):425.

Pollock, John C. Hudson Taylor and Maria: Pioneers in China. New York: McGraw-Hill, Inc., 1962; reprint ed., Grand Rapids: Zondervan Publishing House, 1976.

Principles and Practice of the Overseas Missionary Fellowship. Singapore: Overseas Missionary Fellowship, 1968.

Records of the General Conference of the Protestant Missionary in China. Shanghai: American Presbyterian Mission Press, 1877.

Rees, Luther. A personal letter to L. S. Chafer. CAM International archives, 8 August 1923.

Robinson, C. H. A History of Christian Missions. New York: Charles Scribner's Sons, 1915.

Rupert, Marybeth. "The Emergence of the Independent Missionary Agency as an American Institution, 1860-1917." Ph.D. dissertation, Yale University, 1974.

Shank, Ezra A. Fervent in Spirit: The Biography of Arthur J. Bowen. Chicago: Moody Press, 1954.

Spain, Mildred W. And in Samaria. Dallas: The Central American Mission, 1954.

Speer, Robert E. Missionary Principles and Practice. New York: Fleming H. Revell Co., 1902.

Stauffer, M. T., ed. The Christian Occupation of China. Shanghai: China Continuation Committee, 1922.

Stock, Eugene. A History of the Church Missionary Society, 3 vols. London: Gilbert and Rivington, Ltd., 1899.

Student Volunteer Missionary Union. Students and the Missionary Problem: Addresses Delivered at the International Student Missionary Conference, London, 1900. London: Student Volunteer Missionary Union, 1900.

Sundkler, Bengt. The World of Mission. Grand Rapids: William B. Eerdmans Publishing Co., 1965.

Taylor, F. H. These Forty Years. London: Morgan & Scott Ltd., 1905.

Taylor, Dr. and Mrs. Howard. "By Faith": Henry W. Frost and the China Inland Mission. Philadelphia: China Inland Mission, 1938.

_____. Hudson Taylor and the China Inland Mission: The Growth of a Work of God. London: China Inland Mission, 1918.

_____. _Hudson Taylor in Early Years: The Growth of a Soul_. London: China Inland Mission, 1911.

_____. _Hudson Taylor's Spiritual Secret_. Philadelphia: China Inland Mission, 1932.

_____. _J. Hudson Taylor: God's Man in China_. Chicago: Moody Press, 1965.

Taylor, James Hudson. _China's Spiritual Need and Claims_. London: Morgan & Scott Ltd., 1887.

_____. _Retrospect_. London: Religious Tract Society, 1900.

Thompson, Phyllis. _Each to Her Post_. London: Hodder and Stoughton, 1982.

Troutman, Charles H. "Latin American Survey: What Impelled Them to the Field?" _Evangelical Missions Quarterly_ 4 (Summer 1969): 2-6-209.

Trumbull, Charles G. _The Life Story of C. I. Scofield_. New York: Oxford University Press, 1920.

Turner, Fennell P. ed. _Students and the Present Missionary Crisis: Addresses of the Sixth International Convention of the Student Volunteer Movement for Foreign Missions, Rochester, New York, 1910_. New York: Student Volunteer Movement for Foreign Missions, 1910.

_____, ed. _Students and the World-Wide Expansion of Christianity: The Seventh International Convention of the Student Volunteer Movement, 1914_. New York: Student Volunteer Movement for Foreign Missions, 1914.

Wallstrom, Timothy C. _The Creation of a Student Movement to Evangelize the World_. Pasadena, Ca.: William Carey International University Press, 1980.

Warneck, Gustav. _Outline of a History of Protestant Missions from the Reformation to the Present Time_. Translated by George Robson. 7th ed. New York: Fleming H. Revell Co., 1901.

Winter, Ralph D. and Hawthorne, Steven C., eds. _Perspectives on the World Christian Movement: A Reader_. Pasadena, Ca.: William Carey Library, 1981.